"This is the book that I wish I ha[...] has immediately become the first book I will recom[...] seeking an orientation to what they should know. Required reading for anyone aspiring to culturally competent care."

--Matthew D. Skinta, PhD, ABPP, assistant professor, Roosevelt University, Chicago, IL and author of Contextual Behavior Therapy for Sexual and Gender Minority Clients

"This book fills a huge gap in the field, providing comprehensive perspective on the experience of transgender individuals across the lifespan. It belongs on a reachable bookshelf so that it can be accessed easily and often!"

–Christopher R. Martell, PhD, ABPP, author of Cognitive-Behavioral Therapies with Lesbian, Gay, and Bisexual Clients *and editor of the "Clinician's Digest" in the journal* Psychology of Sexual Orientation and Gender Identity

"A direct yet nuanced and honest call to competent clinical care. Truly a desktop resource for years to come!"

–Sarah Burgamy, PsyD, PhoenixRISE, Denver, CO

"This book reads like a novel while teaching essential lessons to professionals, administrators, and others encountering trans/non-binary individuals. lore portrays realistic and complex life situations masterfully interwoven with applied research, principles of care, and insightful pragmatism in supporting and affirming trans/gender diverse people and their loved ones.

(As a trans man, practicing psychologist, and educator,) I thank you, lore, for addressing a wide scope of issues plus varied roles and demands for professionals while illuminating many experiences of intersectionality."

–Ren Massey, PhD, licensed psychologist, former President, Georgia Psychological Association and adjunct assistant professor, Department of Psychiatry and Behavioral Sciences, Emory University School of Medicine, Faculty, WPATH Global Education Initiative

"Integrates the most advanced knowledge of our fields with the personal experiences of gender diversity using a brilliant range of clients, mental health professionals, and social locations. dickey and his team of experts are the guides so many mental health professionals and students have been hoping to find to support their work with transgender, non-binary, and gender diverse clients and their families."

–Melissa J. Grey, PhD, professor of Psychology, Monroe County Community College and staff psychologist, Integrative Empowerment Group, Saniyah Center, Ypsilanti, MI

of related interest

Supporting Transgender Autistic Youth and Adults
A Guide for Professionals and Families
Finn V. Gratton, LMFT, LPCC
Illustrated by Harper Cheaney
ISBN 978 1 78592 803 1
eISBN 978 1 78450 830 2

ACT for Gender Identity
The Comprehensive Guide
Alex Stitt, LMHC
ISBN 978 1 78592 799 7
eISBN 978 1 78450 812 8

Counseling Transgender and Non-Binary Youth
The Essential Guide
Irwin Krieger
ISBN 978 1 78592 743 0
eISBN 978 1 78450 482 3

Counselling Skills for Working with Gender Diversity and Identity
Michael Beattie and Penny Lenihan with Robin Dundas
ISBN 978 1 78592 741 6
eISBN 978 1 78450 481 6

A Clinician's Guide to Gender Identity and Body Image
Practical Support for Working with Transgender
and Gender-Expansive Clients
Heidi Dalzell, PsyD, CEDS and Kayti Protos, MSW, LCSW
ISBN 978 1 78592 830 7
eISBN 978 1 78450 971 2

Case Studies in Clinical Practice with Trans and Gender Non-Binary Clients

A Handbook for Working with Children, Adolescents, and Adults

lore m. dickey, PhD, ABPP

Foreword by Marsha Botzer

Jessica Kingsley Publishers
London and Philadelphia

First published in Great Britain in 2021 by Jessica Kingsley Publishers
An Hachette Company

1

Copyright © lore m. dickey 2021
Foreword copyright © Marsha Botzer 2021

Front cover image source: Freepik.

*The information contained in this book is not intended to replace the services
of trained medical professionals or to be a substitute for medical advice. You
are advised to consult a doctor on any matters relating to your health, and in
particular on any matters that may require diagnosis or medical attention.*

A CIP catalogue record for this title is available from the
British Library and the Library of Congress

ISBN 978 1 78775 193 4
eISBN 978 1 78775 194 1

Printed and bound in the United States by Integrated Books International

Jessica Kingsley Publishers' policy is to use papers that are natural,
renewable and recyclable products and made from wood grown in
sustainable forests. The logging and manufacturing processes are expected
to conform to the environmental regulations of the country of origin.

Jessica Kingsley Publishers
Carmelite House
50 Victoria Embankment
London EC4Y 0DZ

www.jkp.com

I would like to dedicate this book to the many people who journeyed to understand their gender before I did. Your path was certainly rockier than the one I traveled. I also dedicate this to the people in the trenches working to make this world safe for trans and non-binary people. You are all warriors.

To the people who have inspired me to keep walking toward the light even when I could not see it. Depression and anxiety have, at times, been debilitating for me, and is when I am most creative. I dedicate this to the many people who have propped me up, held my hand, whispered words of kindness, and worked to ensure I can continue to show up in life. My path to this point has been anything but smooth. I love my work; most especially, I love watching you–other trans people–take initial steps to realize yourself as a gendered person. Thank you for letting me witness your journey. Most of all, I want to thank my immediate family: my mother, Dorothy P. McKinney; my sister, Nancy Milstedt; and my brothers, Scott and Tod McKinney. There are lots of nieces and nephews, spouses, and grandnieces and grandnephews.

To Jenny, Jane (both of you), Nancy, Michelle, Ron, Heather, Bruce, and Nicole–I have learned to love myself, to trust my immediate reactions, although this still needs work–to let others love me, and to learn that what I think should be secret (private) is really nothing more than a variation of a human experience. I do that best with my kittens–Hugh, St. Ray, Issy, Nixy, Rusty, and Patch–three male and three female cats–and yet, they are all gender-neutral–having been "fixed." Namasté.

Contents

Foreword by Marsha Botzer. 9

Acknowledgments. 11

Disclaimer 12

Expert Acknowledgment and Biographies 13

Introduction 21

Part One: Childhood

1. Early Childhood. 27

2. Time to Go to School 36

3. Co-occurring Concerns in Childhood:
   Understanding Autism 42

4. Mixed Parental Support. 50

Part Two: Adolescence

5. Puberty, or Why Is My Body Betraying Me? 59

6. Co-occurring Concerns in Adolescence:
   Cutting and Suicidality 66

7. Non-Binary Identities 74

8. Bullying 83

9. Trans Youth and Social Media. 90

10. Sexuality Exploration 100

Part Three: Adulthood

11. Workplace Issues 109

12. Becoming a Trans Parent 117

13. Intersecting Identities 122

14. Military Service Members and Veterans 128

15. Coming Out to Your Children 136

16. Religious Values and Trans Identities 143

17. The Cisgender Partner 150

18. Institutions. 156

19. Advocating for Medical Needs. 163

20. Summary and Conclusion 173

Endnotes 175

Appendix A: Trans Conferences and Other Organizations. . . 176

Appendix B: Sample Letters of Referral 177

Appendix C: Resources for Active Duty, Reserve, and Veteran Service Members 180

Appendix D: Medical Resources 183

References. 184

Further Reading and Other Resources 196

Subject Index. 199

Author Index 205

Foreword

We often meet each other by chance or need. In some instances, those meetings reverberate through the rest of our personal or professional lives, bringing experiences unexpected, and those experiences are revealed only through living out the relationships.

I am so glad I met lore dickey many years ago during work with Ingersoll Gender Center, the organization I founded in the late 1970s. Here was a person looking to blend professional education with lived experience, and to place the results in service to our trans and gender nonconforming communities. Many people have wanted to do this, a brave few have done it, and fewer still have done it as well as lore. You will see the results in this book.

Once, during those long-ago years, I met with a family whose concern was with one child's gender identity. This was before any of the language we have today, and a time when any counselor or therapist who offered help might find themselves ostracized by their professional community. A struggle raged between the parents, one accepting the situation, one not accepting. I wish lore's book could fly back in time to that moment and offer the section that discusses exactly this issue! It all worked out well for the child and the parents, but the information and guidance this book offers would have helped so very much.

Today, professional providers know that the list of concerns and challenges involved in questions of gender and identity is long. Hard personal and academic work has shown specific issues appear regularly, and we now have books that inquire into many of the challenges.

The brilliant move in this book is lore's pairing so many forms of answer with each of the highlighted questions. There are case studies, but there are also stories. There are follow-up discussions of cases, and there are clear sets of recommendations based on the best available knowledge. And, wonderfully, lore has included in each section *additional* analysis by a powerful array of expert providers who follow each specific section with their own comments about the case or issue discussed. This process offers us a chance to learn from a dialogue among colleagues and an opportunity to hear the strong message that we are not alone in facing difficult professional challenges.

Today there is a whole world in conversation about gender, gender identity, and gender expression. For me it comes to this: How can real help and real service be offered to people in immediate and long-term need? What helps the most, harms the least, advances everyone involved, and does the good work honorably and gracefully? This book, and the caring work of lore dickey, are two answers I proudly suggest to you.

With love and respect,

Marsha Botzer
Founder
Ingersoll Gender Center
Seattle, WA

Acknowledgments

Writing, for me, can be a lonely process. One of the reasons is the need to concentrate on what I want to see on the page. For this book, there are many people I need to thank for helping shape the message in each of the cases. On the following pages you will find a list of the people whom I reached out to in order to add their expertise to this work.

I remember as a child thinking about writing a book about my life. Although this is not that book (still a work in progress), this is the first book for which I have been solely responsible for the content. In the past, I have struggled to feel confident in my writing skills. I vividly recall the support I received in graduate school as I struggled to meet the expectations of faculty members. However, one voice from that time is still the loudest when I become discouraged. Even though I have little contact with her today, I thank Jane, from the bottom of my heart, for everything she has done for me. Thank you hardly seems enough to express my gratitude for the years of listening and support. I do not really know another way to say how much you have meant in my life.

Disclaimer

The cases presented in this book may feel non-affirming on some level. In some chapters I introduce a client who has yet to claim their gender identity as being different to the sex they were assigned at birth. Until a client comes to understand their gender identity, I may use the name and pronouns that are consistent with the sex they were assigned at birth. This is not meant to be disrespectful, rather to help the reader understand some of the tension that exists as a client explores their identity.

Each of the cases was created by the author. There may be similarities to the lives of actual people; however, these cases are works of fiction. Any resemblance to a person's lived experience is coincidental.

Expert Acknowledgment and Biographies

This book includes expert commentary for each case. People whose work I greatly respect were asked to write a reaction to the case. These people were encouraged to challenge what had already been written so that we might dispel common myths. Following are short biographies of each expert, alphabetical by first name.

Addis Green, BA (he/him/his) is a Twin Cities-raised, Chicago-based youth worker. He is guided by black, queer, feminist tradition and the belief that abolition is a daily practice. In his current position, he coordinates care at Howard Brown Health for transgender and gender expansive minor-aged youth interested in medically transitioning. When he's not talking about trans things, he is spending time with his cat and listening to house music and early '90s hip-hop.

Alison Cerezo, PhD (she/her/hers; they/them/their) is an assistant professor in the Department of Counseling, Clinical, and School Psychology at UC Santa Barbara. Her primary line of research centers on reducing social and health disparities for sexually and gender diverse communities. Most recently, her work has focused on the links between stigma, discrimination, and substance use as well as reducing barriers to mental health treatment for this community. Alison's scholarly work is rooted in an intersectional and critical race theory perspective, always cognizant of the ways systems of power impact health outcomes and can thus be changed to better support underserved communities.

Benjamin Morsa, PsyD (he/him/his) is a licensed clinical psychologist in private practice in Berkeley, CA, where he provides psychotherapy and psychological assessment services to children and adults. He completed his doctoral training in the George Washington University Professional Psychology Program and is a candidate at the Psychoanalytic Institute of Northern California. His experience includes providing therapy and assessment services in schools and community mental health settings as well as outpatient settings to children and adults, in English and Spanish, from queer, trans, and neurodivergent communities.

Cesar A. Gonzalez, PhD, LP, ABPP (he/him/his; they/them/their) holds a PhD in multicultural community-clinical psychology. Dr. Gonzalez completed his research and clinical postdoctoral fellowship in human sexuality at the University of Minnesota, where he specialized in transgender health. Dr. Gonzalez is board-certified as a clinical psychologist and holds academic appointments as an assistant professor in psychology and family medicine at Mayo Clinic in Rochester, MN. He serves as Clinical Director of Mayo Clinic's Transgender and Intersex Specialty Care Clinic and as an associate program director of the Family Medicine Residency Program.

Christopher Allen, PhD (he/him/his) is an early career psychologist passionate about serving ethnic minorities and marginalized populations in rural and urban Oklahoma. He has gained cultural competence working with Native and African Americans, college students, the aging, adolescents with problematic sexual behavior, adjudicated youth, and incarcerated adults. He has experience working with groups and individuals and providing assessment for children, adolescents, and adults in various settings. These include community mental health, group homes, universities, prisons, tribal clinics, and private practice. He currently provides psychological services to veterans in Tulsa, Oklahoma. Christopher dedicates a substantial portion of his practice to the LGBTQIA community.

Finn V. Gratton, LMFT, LPCC (they/them/their) is a somatic psychotherapist working in the San Francisco Bay Area. Finn's work is focused on the intersections of trauma, neurodiversity, and sexual and gender minorities. They are the author of *Supporting Transgender Autistic Youth and Adults: A Guide for Professionals and Families.*

Jacob Eleazer, PhD (he/him/his) is a postdoctoral psychology fellow in LGBTQ+ Health and Psychosocial Rehabilitation at the Connecticut VA Healthcare System and the Yale School of Medicine. Jacob served in the United States Army National Guard for 12 years and was among the first actively serving transgender soldiers to come out publicly in 2014. Jacob is the Director of Advocacy for SPART*A, a non-profit organization providing social support and advocacy for transgender U.S. service members. After completing the clinical fellowship, Jacob will continue his efforts to improve VA care for the LGBTQ+ veteran community as an advanced postdoctoral fellow in Health Service Research and Development.

Jennifer A. Vencill, PhD (she/her/hers) is an assistant professor, licensed psychologist, and AASECT-certified sex therapist at the Mayo Clinic, where she practices in the Menopause and Women's Sexual Health and Transgender and Intersex Specialty Care clinics. Her clinical and research interests include sexual health and functioning, sexuality and aging, gender and sexual identity development, health disparities and minority stress in marginalized sexual and gender communities, and LGBTQ+ sexual health. Dr. Vencill received her PhD in counseling psychology from Texas Tech University and completed her postdoctoral fellowship at the University of Minnesota Medical School's Program in Human Sexuality.

Jennifer J. Muehlenkamp, PhD (she/her/hers) is a licensed clinical psychologist and professor of psychology at the University of Wisconsin-Eau Claire. Dr. Muehlenkamp is an internationally respected expert on nonsuicidal self-injury (NSSI) and suicide in adolescents and young adults. She is a co-author of two books focused on the assessment and treatment of NSSI and is a regular consultant to mental and behavioral health professionals in her region. Dr. Muehlenkamp's work has been honored with awards from the American Association of Suicidology, over $2 million in research grants, and she is past president of the International Society for the Study of Self-Injury.

Karisa Barrow, PsyD (she/her/hers) is a licensed clinical psychologist who specializes in providing services to gender and sexually diverse children, their families, and adults. She is the founder and executive director of inMind Care, a group practice that provides a range of services for gender and sexually diverse youth, adults, and their families in the Sacramento and Bay Areas in California. She is also a founding member of Mind the Gap, the UCSF Child and Adolescent Gender Center consortium for training gender specialists. Dr. Barrow has been a leading expert in the field for over 20 years and has most recently authored a chapter entitled "Addressing Mental Health Conditions Often Experienced in Transgender and Gender Expansive Youth" in *The Gender Affirmative Model: An Interdisciplinary Approach to Supporting Transgender and Gender Expansive Children* (APA 2018) edited by Colt Keo-Meier and Diane Ehrensaft.

Katie Spencer, PhD, LP, CST (she/her/hers) is an assistant professor, licensed psychologist, certified sex therapist, Co-Director of the National Center for Gender Spectrum Health, and Director of Advocacy and Public Policy at the Program in Human Sexuality at the University of Minnesota. Her primary clinical practice is working with transgender and gender nonconforming adolescents and adults, women's sexuality and sexual health, and LGBTQ+ sexuality and well-being. Dr. Spencer has written, presented, and published scholarship on transgender sexuality, queer femininities, and gender affirmative approaches to transgender healthcare. She provides training and education of therapists and medical providers in sexual health and transgender healthcare competency.

Kelly Ducheny, PsyD (she/her/hers; they/them/their) is a licensed psychologist and the Senior Advisor, Education and Clinical Practice at Howard Brown Health, an LGBTQ federally qualified health center in Chicago, IL. Dr. Ducheny completed a postdoctoral fellowship in integrated care at the Center for Healthy Communities at Wright State University and was a member of the American Psychological Association Task Force that developed the APA *Guidelines for Psychological Practice with Transgender and Gender Nonconforming People*. Dr. Ducheny completed the SAMHSA-HRSA Center for

Integrated Health Solutions Health Disparities Leadership Program in 2012, was a primary investigator on a five-year HRSA SPNS grant exploring engagement and retention of transgender women of color in HIV care, and is a writing group member for the Adult Assessment chapter of the WPATH Standards of Care Version 8.

Kevin Nadal, PhD (he/him/his) is a professor of psychology at John Jay College of Criminal Justice and The Graduate Center at the City University of New York. His numerous leadership positions include former executive director of the CLAGS: The Center for LGBTQ at the Graduate Center; past president of the Asian American Psychological Association; the founder of the LGBTQ Scholars of Color Network; and national trustee of the Filipino American National Historical Society. He has published over one hundred works on multicultural issues, including nine books such as *Microaggressions and Traumatic Stress* (APA 2018) and *Queering Law and Order: LGBTQ Communities and the Criminal Justice System* (Lexington 2020).

Kinton Rossman, PhD (they/them/their) is a psychologist at Howard Brown Health in Chicago, IL. Kinton grew up in rural Kentucky and they identify as white, non-binary, queer, and non-disabled. Along with Addis Green, Kinton helps youth under 18 and their families access gender-affirming, transition-related medical services at Howard Brown Health. Kinton's background includes research on the intersection of health and LGBTQ identity, especially with transgender/gender diverse populations. Kinton is proud to be a parent, partner, and squirrel enthusiast.

Landon Marchant, BA (they/them/their) is a veteran of the United States Air Force, former skilled trades apprentice, community college student, and graduate of Williams College. Motivated by the desire to improve LGBTQ veteran outcomes, Landon has dedicated themselves to providing veterans with the resources, opportunity, and support necessary for post-military success. Their work ranges from direct mentorship and resource-sharing to public speaking, writing, and research. Landon is a founding member of the active-duty transgender military group SPART*A, is a Point Foundation alum (2017–2020), and has performed extensive research examining the individual experiences and collective standpoint of transgender military service members and veterans.

Laura Edwards-Leeper, PhD (she/her/hers) is clinical child psychologist and associate professor in the School of Graduate Psychology at Pacific University in Hillsboro, OR. She was the founding psychologist for the Gender Management Service at Boston Children's Hospital. She has served on national and international committees focused on transgender youth, including the APA task force that developed the *Guidelines for Psychological Practice with Transgender and Gender Nonconforming People* and the SAMHSA committee that created a consensus regarding the danger of conversion therapy. She currently serves as the chair of the WPATH Child/Adolescent Committee and is a member of the youth workgroups revising the Standards of Care. She is an international expert in this area.

Linda Gromko, MD (she/her/hers) is a board-certified family physician and founder of Seattle's Queen Anne Medical Associates. Initially focusing on women's health and obstetrics, the practice added its transgender focus in 1998. When a prospective client asked if she treated transgender women, Dr. Gromko answered, "not yet." She now treats transgender people from ages 5 through 85. In addition to hormone management and peri-operative trans care, Dr. Gromko is a frequent speaker for professional groups. She wrote *Where's MY Book? A Guide for Transgender and Gender Non-Conforming Youth, Their Parents, and Everyone Else*, as well as *A Practical Guide for Transgender and Gender Non-Conforming Adults*.

Michael L. Hendricks, PhD, ABPP (he/him/his) is a partner at the Washington Psychological Center, P.C., in Washington, DC; board-certified in clinical psychology; licensed in DC, Maryland, and Virginia; and a clinical professor at George Washington University's psychology department. He is a fellow of the American Psychological Association, a certified provider by WPATH, and on the editorial board of two professional journals. Dr. Hendricks is the first author on the seminal paper on a minority stress model for trans people. He has taught numerous workshops and trainings on minority stress and mental health work with trans and non-binary people.

Michele Angello, PhD (she/her/hers) works with trans* youth and adults. She offers individual, couples, group, and family therapy, as well as corporate education and training on a variety of issues of sexuality, and she has presented internationally. She offers sessions to people around the world via webcam. Dr. Angello has appeared as an expert on *Dr. Phil, Larry King Live, The Tyra Banks Show, ABC Primetime, Dr. Oz,* and other television shows and documentaries including the award-winning film *TRANS.* She is an adjunct professor in the graduate program of the Center for Sexuality Studies at Widener University in Pennsylvania and developed the first graduate course in the U.S. that focused on clinical issues in transgender communities. She is also a trainer for the Advanced Training for Transgender Communities program through Widener University. Her second book, *Raising the Transgender Child: A Complete Guide for Parents, Families and Caregivers* (Seal Press) came out in 2016.

Mira Jourdan, PhD, ABPP (she/her/hers) is a board-certified neuropsychologist and consultant in private practice. She completed her doctoral training at the University of Florida, internship training at the University of Chicago, and fellowship training at Mary Free Bed Rehabilitation Hospital in Grand Rapids, MI. She is a clinical adjunct faculty member in psychiatry at Michigan State University. She served as the 2020–2021 President of the Society for the Psychology of Sexual Orientation and Gender Diversity (Division 44 of the American Psychological Association). Her areas of specialization include autism, traumatic brain injury, and supporting organizations in embracing diversity, including via professional education on gender and sexual diversity. She identifies as trans and as a woman, is the daughter of Indian immigrants, and is the wife of a trans man, Teri. They reside in Grand Rapids, MI with their cat, Iago.

Ruben Hopwood, MDiv, PhD (he/him/his) is a licensed psychologist working with gender diverse communities and has been educating and training medical and mental health professionals since 2006. He is founder and director of the Cambridge, MA firm Hopwood Counseling & Consulting, LLC, a visiting researcher at The Danielsen Institute at Boston University, and former manager of the Fenway Health Trans Health Program from 2007–2019. Dr. Hopwood is a nationally known speaker, educator, and published author with peer-reviewed journal articles and book chapters on mental health and medical care of gender diverse people, aging and gender diversity, and integrating spiritually into psychotherapy.

Shawn V. Giammattei, PhD (he/him/his) is a clinical psychologist in private practice in Northern California specializing in couple and family therapy with people across the lifespan, with a particular focus on trans youth and their families. He is a researcher, educator, and professor teaching graduate and post-graduate courses in LGBTQ+ psychology and family systems. He is the founder/director of the Gender Health Training Institute, serves on the board of local and national family therapy organizations, is an active member of Mind the Gap, is a WPATH GEI SOC7 Certified Member/Mentor, and is the author of several articles and book chapters on gender, sexuality, and family work.

Tyson L. Pankey, PhD, MPH (he/him/his) is a clinical health psychology fellow at the Mayo Clinic in Rochester, MN. On fellowship, he has a dual emphasis in family medicine residency education and transgender and intersex health. He completed his undergraduate degrees at the University of North Carolina at Chapel Hill and his Master of Public Health degree at the University of Kansas School of Medicine and Public Health. He completed his doctoral degree in counseling psychology from the University of Wisconsin-Madison. As a clinician and researcher, Dr. Pankey is dedicated to addressing health disparities among minoritized populations, including racial/ethnic minorities and LGBTQ+ individuals.

Introduction

Mental health providers have worked with transgender people for many years. Early work with the community followed a gatekeeper model. As a gatekeeper, the mental health provider represented the obstacle between the trans person and their access to life saving care. Too often, the gatekeeper abused the power and expected trans people to conform to an identity story fitting a cisgender, heteronormative ideal. This story met the needs of the provider(s), but it did not address the needs of the trans person in a way that affirmed and supported their felt identity. At the time of the emergence of medical treatment of trans people (the early 1900s), surgeons and physicians risked their livelihood if they were found to remove "healthy tissue." These laws, called "mayhem" laws, were initially enacted in the United Kingdom, because men were undergoing surgery to amputate a part of their body thereby making themselves ineligible to serve in the military (dickey 2020b).

We are far beyond this historical need for mental health providers to serve as a gatekeeper. It is true some people who would like to make a medical transition have some needs to be addressed prior to a medical intervention. However, the vast majority of trans people are not in need of counseling. Although surgeons, physicians, and insurance companies may still require a letter of referral, there is no need to unnecessarily prolong that process.

Today, trans people are more likely to talk about their identity in a way that is consistent with who they are as a gendered (or not) person. Labels that trans people have used for themselves include trans woman, trans man, genderqueer, gender non-binary, gender creative, gender expansive, male, female, agender, and so many more. The ability to talk about one's true identity removes unnecessary barriers in the clinical space so the trans client will talk about concerns that truly matter, rather than trying to meet an arbitrary representation of being trans.

In this book I explore clinical examples of the lived experiences of trans people across the lifespan. I begin in childhood with several clinical scenarios including the need for parental support and the challenges associated with attending school. In the adolescent section I address issues of puberty, self-injury, and discussions of family planning. Finally, in the adult section I address concerns including employment issues, military service, institutional care, and having intersecting identities.

But first, a primer of important definitions and concepts.

Gender–gender is a socialized construct with no biological basis. It is an idea with expectations for how a person should behave based on their perceived sex. Of course, perception of a person's sex can be wrong. Prior to my medical transition, I was often perceived as a man, especially in the women's restroom. Since my medical transition, I am often perceived as a woman based on some combination of the pitch of my voice and my name. These mistakes are a reminder that I need to act in a certain way to satisfy the expectations of society. Gender has both roles and rules. A person who is assumed to be female (sex) must therefore act in a feminine manner lest the gender police correct her errant behavior. The same is true when a person is deemed to be male (sex); however, the consequences for eschewing masculine behavior can be far more significant. It is not the purpose of this book to explore gender roles in great detail. Readers are encouraged to check the Further Reading and Other Resources section at the end of this book for more resources on the topic of gender roles.

Most people hold beliefs about their gender consistent with the sex they were assigned at birth. These people are known as *cisgender*. *Transgender* is an umbrella term used to categorize people whose gender is inconsistent with the sex they were assigned at birth (American Psychological Association 2015). The term *transgender* may not fit all people whose gender differs from their birth sex, so it is important to use the labels and terms your client uses. Some transgender people do not care for the term "label" as it holds negative connotations.

In this book I will use the term *trans*–a shorthand term that may or may not be used by your client. However, it is most inclusive of anyone with a trans identity. Acceptance of this term may change in the future, and I reiterate the importance of using language that is consistent with the client's desires. Language changes rapidly–this is especially true for emerging cultures. Although trans people have existed throughout human history (Chang, Singh, and dickey 2018), we continue to see changes in language used to describe trans people. There was a time when tranny, transgendered, transvestite, and berdache were acceptable terms, and it is possible that *trans* will fall out of favor in the future.

Transsexual gained traction in the 1960s. First used by physicians and other providers, the term is rooted in the medical model (dickey 2020b). As such, it assumes a person plans to make a medical transition (e.g., hormones and/or surgery). The medical model also assumed a person would be heterosexual post-transition (Benjamin 1966). Some trans people still use transsexual as it most closely fits their identity.

Although *gender identity* is a person's felt sense of who they are as a gendered individual, *sexual identity* relates to one's attraction to another person(s) or no person at all. Sexual identity traditionally has been further categorized as heterosexual, homosexual, bisexual, and asexual. The term *homosexual* is offensive to many people and it may be better to use *gay* or *lesbian*, based on the client's wishes.

Although sexual and gender identity are not the same, they inform one another. We make assumptions, right or wrong, about a person's sexual identity based on who they are partnered with as well as our beliefs about their gender (identity). This may not be accurate, especially since a person's sexual behavior may not be part of their identity. To understand this concept, we may need to suspend our beliefs about what it means to be a sexual person, as even people who engage in sex with a person may hold an identity inconsistent with their behavior.

Some people have a gender identity consistent with the *gender binary*, a construct best defined as the assumption that there are two, and only two, immutable genders (feminine and masculine). Other people eschew the gender binary and live somewhere along the gender spectrum, as a third gender, as another gender, or no gender at all. People with non-binary identities may use unfamiliar pronouns (e.g., they, them, per, ze, hir, hirself). It is important to use the pronouns that a client uses, regardless of familiarity.

All of these concepts are considered fundamental knowledge for people who work with transgender and gender nonconforming people (American Psychological Association 2015; Chang et al. 2018), as an element of affirmative clinical practice. This may change over time as trans people continue to define their identity.

Affirmative practice is defined as any practice that is "culturally-relevant for TGNC [transgender and gender nonconforming] clients and their multiple social identities, addresses the influence of social inequities on the lives of TGNC clients, enhances TGNC client resilience and coping, advocates to reduce systemic barriers to TGNC mental and physical health, and leverages TGNC client strengths" (Singh and dickey 2017, p.4). In terms of cultural relevance, it is critical to consider intersecting identities in addition to traditionally marginalized identities, which I will address as I consider the various cases presented in this book. Providers must also attend to the social barriers that may impact a trans person's life. Understanding a client's resilience and ability to engage in prosocial coping strategies is critical.

As each year passes, trans people are more present in society and they deserve to be treated with respect and dignity. You may have only one opportunity to correct the misconceptions held by others about how trans people are treated by mental health providers. This book should help you to gain a minimum level of knowledge to ensure you are seen by trans clients as competent to manage their mental health needs.

This book is divided into three sections: childhood, adolescence, and adulthood. Each section has a number of chapters, each of which represents a new case. Unique to this book is that each case includes a short response from an expert familiar with the type of clinical material presented in the chapter. It is my hope that these reactions by experts in the field will help to bring the case material to life.

PART ONE

Childhood

CHAPTER 1

Early Childhood

As early as the age of three, a child may express to their parents that they are not a girl or boy as they were assigned at birth. For most parents, this does not fit with the plans or expectations for their child. The case in this chapter explores a young child's assertion they are not a boy, do not want to use the name they were given at birth, and want to present as a girl in all areas of their life.

Children tend to use different terminology than adults. Instead of *trans* you might hear *gender expansive, gender fluid*, or *gender creative*. In working with adults, you are likely to find they knew there was something different about their life from a young age, even if they did not have the words to describe that difference. It is more common today for children to come out to their parents at young ages. Even though there are no medical interventions for trans children, the gender expansive child may need mental health support. It is critically important to support the child and their parents. We know from research that gender fluid children who are supported by their parents are more likely to have positive outcomes including better grades, improved mental health, and quality interactions with their peers (Olson et al. 2016; Ryan et al. 2010).

Details of the case

In this case we have a four-year-old who was assigned male at birth and given the name Jason. Jason asserts that she wants to be called Jessica. Her parents are Shelly and Jeff. Jessica attends a local day care. The director of the day care center has spoken with Jason's parents on several occasions about "bizarre behavior," including playing with dolls and pretending to be a girl during open play time. This case will be presented using the names and pronouns given at birth until the child asserts otherwise.

Exploring clinical material

You receive a call from a distraught mother, Shelly. She says her four-year-old son asserts he is a girl. She and her husband, Jeff, have been letting their son engage in what they call "girl play" at home but not outside of their home. The child, Jason, is third-generation Japanese. Shelly and Jeff are from the Seattle area and their great grandfathers met one another while in a World War II (WWII) internment camp in Idaho. After being released from the camp, both families relocated to Seattle and remained good friends. Shelly and Jeff's families have attempted to hold on to their Japanese values, though with each generation it seems more cultural values fall by the wayside.

You invite Shelly and Jeff to meet with you, and they arrive on time for the first appointment. As you observe them, you notice quickly that neither wears shoes. Jeff states that in their culture guests are expected to leave their shoes at the door so as not to soil or damage the flooring in the host's residence. This cultural belief is tied closely to Japanese people historically serving their food from the floor (Hendry 1984). By leaving their shoes at the entrance they are exhibiting respect for their host.

You realize how important their respective familial histories are. You typically use a genogram to understand the family and the influences that impact the family system. When creating a genogram for this family, the clients are insistent you include their respective great grandfathers, not just the typical three generations used when creating a genogram. The reason for this is they may never have met if their great grandfathers had not first met in Minidoka, ID during WWII.

Their child, Jason, is the youngest of their three children. Before Jason could talk, Shelly noticed that he was more interested in the clothing of girls and the types of toys that are typically associated with girls. Jason was drawn to his older sister's toys and liked to dress in her clothing. Shelly stated she "attempted to curb that activity early in Jason's life." She was concerned about how Jeff would respond if he ever "caught Jason" engaging in girl play. Although Shelly comes from a culturally conservative family, Jeff's cultural views are even more conservative. It was these conservative values that first brought their families together in Idaho.

Eventually Jeff became aware of Jason's behavior. In addition to punishing Jason, Jeff lashed out at Shelly for allowing Jason to behave in this way. Shelly attempted to deflect his anger by placing the blame on the day care center Jason attended. In the course of the past two years, Jason has attended seven different day care centers. This is due to Jeff's belief, based on Shelly's early comment, that the day care center is where Jason is learning this behavior.

Jeff was reluctant to come to see you even though Shelly insisted he be part of the process. Jeff is five years older than Shelly. They both reported having a wonderful relationship until the past two years, during which it seems all they do is fight. Shelly just wants Jason to be happy. Jeff admits he wants Jason to be happy, too, "as the boy he is."

In session three you ask to meet alone with Shelly. You plan to meet with Jeff the following week. Shelly's demeanor is different. When you ask about this, she states that she just wants Jason to be happy and if that means he plays with dolls, what does that really matter? She also talks about how hard it is to be supportive of Jason when Jeff is at home. She feels like she is sneaking behind Jeff's back in regard to Jason and what he is allowed to do.

The following week you meet with Jeff, whose demeanor and affect are no different than usual. As you explore his feelings about Jason you quickly realize Jeff associates Jason's behavior with being gay. What Jeff is most concerned about is that Jason will "grow up to be gay." Consider the following conversation.

Counselor: It is clear you do not like it when Jason plays with dolls. What worries you most about this behavior?

Jeff: My biggest concern? My biggest concern is that he will grow up to be gay. My mother and my grandparents will not tolerate that from me–that I would let my son be *okama* [Japanese slang term for gay].

Counselor: What if there are other options for Jason? What if Jason is trying to express his feminine side because Jason is really a girl, and not a boy?

Jeff: I'm not sure that is any better than being *okama*. Being *onabe* is not safer than being *okama*. You asked me before about my biggest concern. Well, really, I mostly worry that as Jason grows up, he will be hurt or even killed. [Jeff begins to choke up.]

Counselor: It makes sense you would be concerned about Jason's well-being. I can't imagine a parent that wouldn't be concerned as you are. We've talked in our sessions about the different ways a parent can support their child. One thing we know from research is that children who are supported by their family are more likely to adjust in positive ways to the challenges they face.

Jeff: I guess that makes sense. I really wish I could predict how this will turn out. I love Jason dearly, and I want the best for him. I just have a hard time seeing how all of this will work out.

As the session comes to an end, you ask Jeff if he will bring Jason and Shelly to the next appointment. You want the chance to talk directly with Jason to get a better sense of what this means for him. From your previous work with children, you know they usually will communicate more freely if they are playing while talking. You have a broad assortment of toys in your office for just that purpose.

You start the session with both parents in the room, engaging with each of the family members to help Jason feel safe. Jason is shy and reluctant to engage. He spends most of his time cuddled up to his mother. This behavior is consistent with his age.

During the next session, it seems Jason is becoming more comfortable with you. You ask Jason if he will play a game with you and his parents. He picks out the game Candy Cane Lane and the four of you play. Jason is absorbed by the game. In the follow-up session, Jason agrees to meet with you without his parents present. In your conversation with Jason he quietly asks if you will use the name Jessica and the pronouns she/her/hers. You agree and tell Jessica you might make a mistake and that you will correct yourself. Jessica understands this. You then ask her if she has ever shared this with her parents. She slowly nods her head. Through tears she asks you not to say anything to her parents because they will get mad at her. Although there is no imminent danger to Jessica, you are concerned about keeping secrets. Over time, Jessica feels more confident about her identity and is able to talk about it with her parents. Jeff also comes to see how supporting Jessica will be helpful in the long run. Shelly is supportive and makes time to be with Jessica, as Jessica, each day.

General commentary

When working with pre-school-aged children it is important to be supportive without being directive. Children this age can be impressionable. If there is a "wait and see" time period for minor children, this would be it. Parents, and a mental health provider, can be supportive while still waiting to see if the child has a trans identity.

Keo-Meier and Ehrensaft (2018) propose the Gender Affirmative Model (GAM). The model is based on the following theoretical notions:

a. gender identity or expression must not be pathologized;

b. gender expression is diverse and may differ depending on a person's cultural identity; this requires cultural humility;

c. leaders in the field of work with trans people believe that gender identity is a combination of biology, development, socialization, culture, and context;

d. gender whether fluid or not, is inclusive of multiple gender identities; gender identity may change over time; and

e. mental health concerns are more likely to be related to cultural reactions to gender diversity (e.g., transphobia, homophobia, sexism) and not because of the child's personality.

Some of these notions deserve elaboration. First, no gender or gender identity is pathological. Many medical organizations (e.g., American Medical Association, American Association of Pediatrics) have published statements that people with trans identities should not be pathologized. The primary means of pathologization is the use of a mental health disorder (e.g., gender dysphoria; *Diagnostic and Statistical Manual of Mental Disorders* [DSM], American Psychiatric Association 2013) to determine eligibility for transition-related care. Although the diagnosis of gender dysphoria is more favorable than gender identity disorder (from the *DSM-IV Text Revision*, American Psychiatric Association 2000), there are still problems with this diagnosis.

Second, gender is on a spectrum; it is not a binary construct (American Psychological Association 2015). Although most people see only boy/girl or male/female options, the truth is a person can identify anywhere along the spectrum. Gender is also fluid. This means one's gender identity may change over their lifetime. This can be difficult for providers and loved ones, but the challenge should be addressed head-on and not made the client's concern.

Finally, gender can vary across cultural backgrounds. In one culture it may be acceptable to have an androgynous identity. Some cultures are supportive of third or fourth gender individuals. In fact, some cultures see people with a third gender as healers or as holding a sacred position within the community (dickey 2020a).

Research has shown some children who express "cross-sex"[1] behaviors at a young age grow up to be gay. That is not going to be the case for all children, some will be straight (heterosexual), and others trans. There are varying approaches for how to work with children.

An affirmative approach to counseling

Using the GAM, you might start with Jessica's parents to gain a deeper understanding of their beliefs about gender. It is important to ascertain the source of those beliefs. Is the source of these beliefs deeply held cultural values? Do they come from their own upbringings as male/female? Did the parents learn about gender during their formative years based on how their peers interacted with them? It is likely all of these sources influence Shelly and Jeff's beliefs. To the extent cultural values play a part in their lives, it is important not to make assumptions based on stereotypes about Japanese people. Allow Shelly and Jeff to explain how this fits without foreclosing on your own knowledge.

It is common for parents to think they have "done something wrong" in raising their children. We saw this when Jeff lashed out at Shelly for allowing Jessica to engage in "girl play." Shelly might easily internalize Jeff's anger and assume she is responsible for how Jessica behaves. The GAM posits there are many influences, including biology, development, and culture, that affect how a child develops (Keo-Meier and Ehrensaft 2018). None of these influences is solely responsible for the way a child expresses their gender.

Although this does not appear to be the case for Jessica, it is possible a child will present with a fluid gender. This means from day to day they express their gender differently or they have a non-binary identity. In these cases, it is possible children will ask people to use non-binary pronouns (e.g., they/them/their; ze; hir). The challenge for most people is not only learning that these pronoun options exist, but also incorporating them into their vocabulary.

EXPERT COMMENT

The cultural intersections of this case could make working with this family complicated and very difficult if not addressed up front. Therefore, understanding the culture and values of this family, as outlined in the approach above, is imperative. Also, given this child's age, using the "wait and see" approach is generally a good plan, as even the most adamant children may shift as they age, especially in their preferences for play and dress. At the same time, if we are using the GAM, we will want to follow the child's affirmed identity, supporting her gender health, while holding that this may change. What we must be careful of in this case is writing off Jessica's behavior as a play preference because she is so young and ignoring her current affirmed gender. It is important to remember most children, including trans children, are clear about their identities at age four, so this should not be dismissed or minimized.

Most of the work in this case is with the parents, especially with Jeff coming to understand the influence he can have as a parent on his child's physical and mental health, and working with the couple to come together to support their child; they need to understand there is no neutral option. Given Jeff's reticence to see you and the likelihood he will pull his family out of therapy, you will need to take extra care to join with him. As a part of this joining, in addition to exploring cultural notions around gender and transgressing gender norms, it is important to understand Jeff and Shelly's beliefs around parenting and their role in the development of gender and sexuality. In particular, how does Jeff see his role in this? What happens to his standing in his community or family if he "fails" in this role to produce heterosexual and cisgender offspring? As he comes to embrace his fears for his child, he may feel shame that needs to be addressed so he can meet the needs of his gender expansive child. Another issue this couple will need help facing is their extended families and community, the potential resulting judgments, and losses and safety plans if they publicly support their child's gender. If it is not safe for the family or for Jessica to socially transition outside of the home (if that is what she wants), they may need to come up with some creative ways to affirm her gender while still holding that it might move in a different direction.

For Jessica, individual sessions revealed that her gender expansiveness is much deeper than a preference for toys and clothes, and, according to her mother, the preference for things typical for a girl has been present her whole life, making it consistent, insistent, and persistent, even at the age of four. It is important to explore Jessica's response when Jeff blocked access to feminine toys and clothes as well as the seriousness of her behavior; does the gender play feel like serious work? Or is it something she dons like a costume and then goes back to being Jason? If it is the latter, watchful waiting, while supporting her gender explorations, would be appropriate. If it is the former, then we should work with the parents to make it safe for Jessica to come out to them, and then help Shelly and Jeff follow Jessica's lead.

It is unhealthy for the child and the family for the therapist to collude with the child to keep her affirmed identity a secret from the parents. Hiding comes at a psychological cost for the whole family and can reinforce the thought that this is in fact a terrible thing that needs to be hidden. There is harm when a child does not feel safe to share who they are with their parents. This should be a temporary tactic as a part of creating a safe space in your office, while you work with Shelly and Jeff to find an openness to allow their child to express her true identity rather than foreclosing on it. Their ability to witness and follow their child's lead will build resilience for Jessica and the family and not leave them at a disadvantage if Jessica comes out later as trans.

Expert comment authored by Shawn V. Giammattei, PhD, Santa Rosa, CA

Take-home messages
"Waiting and seeing" how a child experiences their gender may be most appropriate in young children. There is no urgency, outside of the felt gender experience, to move forward. This is not meant to diminish the urgency the child may feel. If the parents remain supportive, this time period will be less disruptive for the child.

Allowing both parents to talk with you on their own terms appears to have made a difference in their ability to come together. Jessica still is not sure if she is safe in expressing her true identity, but as stated, you can keep this between the two of you (for a short time), as there is no danger for Jessica.

CHAPTER 2

Time to Go to School

By the time a child attends school, they realize much of their day is divided based on sex. From restrooms to activities to expected manner of dress, children are, in many ways, assaulted with gendered expectations. These expectations include the types of friends they have, the ways they behave, and the ways they learn. When children are forced to comport themselves in ways that do not fit with their felt sense of identity, the school day can become quite challenging for the child, the teacher, and the child's parents.

Children already have a good sense of their gender by school age. The challenge can be the school system, its policies, and the amount of exposure teachers and staff have had in working with trans students. When parents approach the school seeking an affirmative learning environment, they do not always receive a warm reception. This is one of the times in a trans person's life when they most benefit from having allies, even when those allies are their parents.

Details of the case

Julius is a six-year-old African American. Julius was assigned female at birth and has made a social transition at home. He has relatively positive support from his parents and siblings. They struggle to use the correct pronouns (he/him/his), which upsets Julius. Julius has a small group of friends on the street where his family lives. He was nervous about starting kindergarten because he would be attending a different school than his best friend. Even though his mother was able to calm him down those first few weeks, some days were much harder than others.

Exploring clinical material

You began working with Julius and his family last year when he was in kindergarten. It was midway through the school year and Julius had been talking about being male identified for some time. Julius's mother, LaQuisha, came to see you to try to understand what she had done wrong in raising Julius.

Over the course of several sessions you were able to help LaQuisha to see she had done nothing wrong. She came to understand having a diverse gender identity was natural and that, although she was concerned about Julius's future, being supportive of Julius would help to ensure he would grow up with strong self-confidence and a clear sense of his identity.

LaQuisha shares with you that Julius would like to start using his male name and to dress as a boy in all aspects of his life. She is scared about how fellow students, teachers, and school staff will react. Your conversation goes like this:

LaQuisha: This past weekend Julius had a bit of a meltdown. He insisted that he be able to be Julius in school and everywhere else, including church. She—I mean he—said he hates wearing dresses and will destroy them if he has to wear one again.

Counselor: It sounds like he has a clear sense of himself. What are the concerns about moving forward? We have been talking about this for some time now.

LaQuisha: I know, but now that the time is here, I'm just so scared for him and for our family. We live in a pretty conservative neighborhood and I just don't know how our neighbors will respond.

Counselor: What is the worst possible reaction they might have?

LaQuisha: Hurting Julius would be high on the list. I also worry that our house or cars will be vandalized. Then at school, I wonder if the teachers will be supportive.

Counselor: It sounds like you have a number of concerns. Let's start with the first one—that Julius might be hurt. Is there someone in particular you are concerned about?

LaQuisha: No, not really. It is just that our experience with Julius is so different than what other families are going through. I know he is young, but that does not mean someone won't hurt him. He is small for his age, especially given that he was assigned female at birth.

Counselor: In what ways do you imagine you can protect him?

LaQuisha: Hmmm, I guess that instead of having him go to his friends' houses they could come to our house. That way I can keep an eye on what is going on and stop things from escalating if need be.

Counselor: That is a good idea. Anything else you might do?

LaQuisha: Well, I've been thinking about inviting our closest friends in the neighborhood over for dinner. Besides having a nice social experience, I would use the dinner as time to let them know what is going on with Julius. I know that my friends Jackson and Shirley will be supportive, and I can let them know what the dinner is about ahead of time. That way, they can help be supportive.

Counselor: You have really thought this out. It seems like you already have some good ways to respond to the concerns about Julius's safety.

LaQuisha: I guess so...

The conversation can continue to address the other concerns LaQuisha has. It is important to address issues within the family as well.

School concerns

LaQuisha brings Julius to the next session. You notice he has a black eye. LaQuisha reports that he got into a fight on the playground and has been suspended from school. The worst part for LaQuisha is that the playground monitors did not intervene. Julius felt attacked by the other child and now he does not want to go back to school after his suspension has been completed. Julius is in tears in your office as he recounts what happened. The issue began in his first period class. He tried to ignore the other student, but at recess, the student began following him around the playground saying mean things to him. Eventually the boy began to throw rocks at Julius. Julius tried to walk away but the other boy escalated the altercation. The worst part is Julius felt all alone and the playground monitors did not intervene.

You and LaQuisha work to calm Julius down without ignoring his real concerns. You talk to LaQuisha about the ways you can help her interact with the school administration. You make a plan to work with LaQuisha at your next appointment on how to have a conversation with school officials as you want to be sure Julius is feeling supported and has his emotional and physical safety needs met.

As you focus on Julius, he says the fight on the playground is not the only issue. Last week his class was going to an assembly in the cafeteria and the teacher asked them to line up with the boys on the left and the girls on the right. At first, Julius was not sure which line to get in. He had always used the girls' line before. That day he decided it would be alright to use the boys' line. In his mind, he was a boy and since he was dressed as a boy he should be lined up with the boys. Unfortunately, his teacher did not see things the same way. His teacher called out to Julius that "she needed to be in the girls' line." This did not end well for Julius in part because the other children began laughing. Julius put his head down and did not look at anyone the rest of the day.

These types of experiences are not uncommon for school-aged children. They have not developed the maturity to understand how adults view things. As a result, their response to adults may fall far short of their intended mark. Although you can likely expect this type of occurrence, it is possible you cannot fully prepare the child and their parents for every eventuality. If you work regularly with children, you may want to keep your own list of the types of concerns your clients bring. Having thought through some of these issues will help you be better prepared to address them with your clients. You also are in a place where you can see patterns in the community where you work. If you know a particular school has a hostile administration, you will help your clients by letting them know.

Working with school administrators

A number of issues can arise in school. GLSEN and the National Center for Transgender Equality (GLSEN and NCTE 2018) have published a document titled *Model School District Policy on Transgender and Gender Nonconforming Students: Model Language, Commentary, and Resources* that covers a broad array of issues that occur in schools. This document is based on the latest information about federal laws in the United States that protect children based on their gender. The document covers federal and safe-school laws, how to address bullying (see Chapter 8 for more information about bullying), privacy and confidentiality, school records, access to gender segregated activities and facilities, dress codes, student transitions, and more. The document is comprehensive and a good resource to have handy in your office and to make known to your clients.

Regardless of concern, it is good practice to reach out to school administrators sooner rather than later. People do not usually like to be surprised and most people who work in school systems have a genuine commitment to the safety and well-being of their students. If you can help them to reasonably foresee possible concerns, they are likely to help address them before any damage is done.

EXPERT COMMENT

There are unique challenges when a person comes out as a minor. The lack of agency can exacerbate the feelings of loneliness; this is known as adultism (Singh 2013). Julius has "relatively positive support from his parents and siblings." Though this is more than many people experience, the conditional love surrounding this is painful and palpable. It is not explicit or overt and his family is obviously doing the best they can, but Julius's initial sharing of his gender identity was met with skepticism and shame. I often wish I could erase the initial reaction a person receives from loved ones because it is often one of shock, disbelief, or even disgust. LaQuisha's concern that she did something to cause Julius to be trans is quite common. As parents, we often feel responsible for aspects of our children, and when these are concepts we are unfamiliar with, we run the risk of responding irrationally.

Planning a gathering of neighbors and friends is a wise way to introduce Julius's new identity to a safe inner circle. The idea of having friends who LaQuisha knows will be supportive have the information ahead of time is good as well. This can ideally take some of the burden of coming out and answering the same questions over and over again off of LaQuisha and her family.

School is a place where all children should feel safe. After the incident at recess, Julius's ability to have confidence that adults were available to ensure his safety was torn from him. Being called out for being in the "wrong" line was humiliating. Ideally the school would have a meeting prior to Julius presenting as male and allow faculty and staff to be appropriately educated and prepared to handle questions from the child's peers or even parents of the peers. In some situations, the children would also be given the opportunity to be educated as a school community or at least in the classroom. When people are given accurate information, they tend to be less likely to intentionally or even inadvertently invalidate the individual who is transitioning. Demystifying the experience can take some of the fear away, which will lessen the likelihood Julius will be confronted by further challenges and allow him to be seen as a resilient child. There was some harm done, which needs to be fixed if he is to feel like he is on equal footing.

Expert comment authored by Michele Angello, PhD, Wayne, PA

Take-home messages

Listen to children. When they express to you that they identify differently than the sex they were assigned at birth, be understanding and help them to figure this out. Assuming a parent "did something wrong" is a trap. Being trans is a normal occurrence. You cannot parent a child in a way that will make them want to change their gender.

Prior to attending school, children learn the rules about gender behavior primarily from their families. Once a child begins school, the rules about gender can be amplified. The amplification may not serve the child if it is based solely on the gender binary. Children attending school in politically and religiously conservative areas may find there are no options outside male/boy or female/girl. All children deserve to live and interact with others in a space that allows them to fully express their gender.

CHAPTER 3

Co-occurring Concerns in Childhood: Understanding Autism

Autism spectrum disorders appear to be increasing in the general population. Prior to the publication of *DSM-5* (American Psychiatric Association 2013) there were two disorders–autism or Asperger's. The fifth edition of the DSM combined these into a single disorder called autism spectrum disorder (ASD). It may be difficult to find a provider who is skilled in both gender dysphoria and ASD (Strang et al. 2016).

Recent research has shown there may be a connection between ASD and trans children, but this is not proof either condition causes the other. Any assumption of causation is flawed and may be harmful to the client. I will later address some of the harm this assumption can cause to clients.

Details of the case

A 12-year-old was assigned male at birth and uses the name Amanda. She asserts she wants to be called Amanda. Amanda's parents are Dwight and Carol. Amanda is in the sixth grade and attends a local junior high. Amanda was diagnosed with ASD in kindergarten. She struggled prior to that, but her parents did not have the resources to send her to a pre-school so ASD was first noticed when she started elementary school.

Exploring clinical material

You are a school counselor and have been working with Amanda since she began school this past fall. Amanda had an Individualized Education Plan (IEP) when she was in grade school. You have been working with Amanda's parents to update the IEP, but they have been uncooperative. Amanda needs an updated assessment to have accommodations in the classroom.

Amanda has been a "B" student. She enjoys math and science. She especially excels at individual projects. She struggles with group projects and often is the last person picked to work with a group as fellow students have a hard time working with Amanda.

Amanda has been presenting as female since the fourth grade. Although her parents have generally been supportive of Amanda, you get the sense that this is not always the case. Consider the following conversation.

Counselor: How have things been going lately?

Dwight: It's hard to say. We've been thinking this was just a phase for Amanda.

Counselor: A phase? In my conversations with Amanda, it sounds like she has thought of herself as a girl for six or more years.

Dwight: I know. I want what is best for my child, but I question whether exploring gender this way is the right choice.

Counselor: You really care about Amanda and yet you are not sure how to proceed, do I understand that correctly?

Dwight: Yes. I'm concerned partly because I struggle to see a real future for my child as a girl.

You are aware Amanda's father is doing all of the talking while her mother has a closed posture and seems either uninterested or indignant. Dwight is usually the parent who attends the parent-teacher conferences and, although he advocates for Amanda's learning needs, he also seems unable to engage Amanda in the type of care that would lead to her best success. You have referred Dwight and Carol to Trans Youth Family Allies, which has a number of online resources for the parents of trans youth.

Two months later, Carol calls you and states she does not want Timothy (the name Amanda was given at birth) to attend the health education class. She states she is concerned her "boy will get the wrong message" and she feels strongly that the information covered in the health education class is the parents' responsibility. She insists "if Timothy is not offered an alternative class activity," she will remove him from the school. You are concerned about Amanda and the messages she is receiving at home. Amanda's grades are beginning to drop, and you have heard reports that she is being bullied because of her autism and her gender.

General commentary

This case is representative of the cumulative effect of intersecting identities. Amanda learned to adjust to the social demands of school through her IEP in grade school. On moving to middle school this plan did not follow her, as it was due for renewal, and the school counselor has struggled to find the best way to meet Amanda's academic needs. Although Amanda has been able to progress through each academic year with her peers, middle school has provided additional challenges, including having difficulty getting to her classroom on time, strained relationships with her peers, and trouble addressing some of her basic needs such as using the bathroom.

In a qualitative research study, Kuvalanka and colleagues (2018) found mothers in their study tended to think gender exploration was part of ASD. However, nowhere in the diagnostic nomenclature will you find "exploring gender" as a phase of ASD. In spite of what some people believe, nothing at this time outside of correlational research implies there is a connection between ASD and gender identity.

An affirmative approach to counseling

Amanda would likely benefit from working with a provider who has experience with both ASD and trans people. This may be difficult to find unless they live in a large city or near a children's hospital with a gender clinic (e.g., Philadelphia, Phoenix, Seattle, Boston). Strang and colleagues (2016) offer guidelines for working with trans youth on the autism spectrum, including recommendations for assessment and treatment, social concerns, medical care, medical safety, risk of victimization, young adulthood, school and employment, and romantic relationships.

Strang and colleagues (2016) recommend trans children be assessed for ASD and vice versa. If you are a provider who specializes in work with trans youth, consider obtaining training in work with youth on the autism spectrum. There are a number of assessment tools for determining if a child is on the autism spectrum including the Autism Spectrum Rating Scale (ASRS) (Goldstein and Naglieri 2009), Childhood Autism Rating Scale (CARS2) (Schopler et al. 2010), and the Gilliam Autism Rating Scale (GARS-3) (Gilliam 2013). The same cannot be said about the presence of validated assessments for gender dysphoria, as they do not exist. A well-trained clinician should have a firm grasp on the diagnostic criteria associated with gender dysphoria and be able to determine whether a child or adolescent meets the diagnostic threshold.

Strang et al. (2016) reinforce the need for an interdisciplinary team, to address the "intensity of gender feelings" (p.6), engage in psychoeducation with the adolescent/child and their parents, and provide structure for the client to explore their gender and the ways it intersects with ASD symptoms. There may be a need for additional parental support depending on the severity of the ASD. Guidelines point to the need for a pediatric endocrinologist on the treatment team, to assure appropriate medical treatment is provided to the child/adolescent. Although there are several other treatment guidelines, it is important to consider the ways the client engages with others in a social context. Strang and colleagues (2016) aptly discuss that a child can be bullied for either autism or their gender identity and that when a child has these co-occurring clinical concerns, the mistreatment can be that much worse.

EXPERT COMMENT

This is a case that highlights some of the deep issues that arise in working with trans autistic youth and their parents. It reveals the impact of stigma upon acceptance and support for both autistic and transgender experiences. Despite their child's long-standing trans identity, Dwight and Carol persist in denying her experience and fail to adequately support her identity, in this case for the stated reason of fear for the child's future as a trans woman.

Parents of autistic children may fear for their child's future as autistic people in a society that stigmatizes and discriminates against them. As parents of a child who was diagnosed in first grade, Dwight and Carol have had seven years to be intensively steeped in the societal pathologiziation of autistic people. They may have internalized beliefs that autistic people are less mature than neurotypical people and that autistics (and everyone) should endeavor to comport ourselves in a neurotypically acceptable way. This extinguishment of autistic presentation and move toward neurotypical presentation is a primary social goal of most treatment programs for autistic people. Dwight and Carol profess real fears that their child will not thrive as a trans woman in this world, a feeling that may align with their fear that their child may not thrive as an autistic person. One defensive strategy to cope with this fear is to do everything possible to reduce autistic symptoms—and another is to deny the need for support and to focus on a child's abilities, in this case, decent grades within mainstream courses. Dwight and Carol, in denying or failing to support both the trans and the autistic non-normative experiences in their child, may be trying to hold back their fears of non-normativity or of reprisal or rejection for their child or their family. This may have been compounded by their experience of their child's IEP process—one that is steeped in the language of deficit and disability.

For Amanda to get the support she needs from her family, her parents will need to do some deep work on their fears and judgments. Although some of this can be done with a therapist, peers who have experienced similar feelings, such as trans family groups, can be very helpful. The challenge here is that Amanda has become significantly more distressed and is in urgent need of support for her trans identity while her parents do not feel the same urgency and are pulling back. It will take the use of a careful intervention with alignment around the parents' love for their child and the current effects and ongoing risks of their low support for and persisting denial of a trans identity to Amanda's mental health. An interdisciplinary team including school therapist, gender specialist physician, gender affirmative parent support group, and family therapist would be helpful if all team members are gender and neurodiversity affirming.

Regarding the IEP, further investigation is needed to understand Amanda and her parents' experience with the past IEP. Parents may be non-responsive because of stigma and denial, and there could be other reasons for their reluctance to engage in assessment. Many children and their parents feel that the IEP interventions have not been very helpful. An exploration of reluctance to participate is in order, as is a willingness to adapt IEP goals and objectives to be the best fit for Amanda. It is important to note that common treatment for autism is to extinguish communication and behavior that is considered uncomfortable to others and to try to instill more normative behavior or communication. This goes directly against the effort of gender care, in which providers support individuals in coming to know and express their authentic experience. Because the authentic expression of autistic people is held as unacceptable, it is not a surprise that the authentic gender identity and expression of autistic people has been called into question.

Humans are prone to confusing correlation and causation. In spite of a correlation between trans and autistic identities, they are not neatly separated because they are intricately, and intimately, at play for trans autistic individuals. This makes the mismatch of affirmation of gender identity and disaffirmation of autistic symptoms a setup for an impossible task for any person and leaves this child vulnerable to psychic splits and her family less equipped to support her.

Researchers have become focused on what is called an "over representation" of autistic people in the transgender population, with estimates ranging from 5–20 percent of trans people being autistic. No one has looked at the overrepresentation of neurotypical people among the cisgender population. Why are so many neurotypical people cisgender? Does the neurotypicality stem from their cisgender experience or vice versa? There are additional concerns with how our current medical system identifies and fails to identify autism. Autism is a diagnosis that is widely missed (or misdiagnosed as another issue) by many professionals, including educators, physicians, and mental health providers, particularly for people of color and people who were assigned female at birth. Screening tools offered in this case are only a first step, and these may miss many people assigned female at birth. Psychologists are increasingly aware that autism has been under-researched and undertheorized when considering people assigned female at birth. They define this topic under the heading "autism in women"—a phenomenon that perpetuates the invisibility of those who live in this intersection. A detailed and comprehensive assessment by a mental health professional trained in discerning different autistic presentations is necessary to more accurately diagnose and provide a more nuanced picture of strengths and challenges for autistic youth and adults, particularly those people who do not fit screening criteria that are biased toward a particular presentation of autism. These assessments are intensive and expensive and experienced providers may not be available in many areas. This is a significant barrier to access. For this reason, along with the all-too-common experience of professionals telling self- and community-identified autistic people that they aren't autistic (because they make eye contact, have empathy, or mask their challenges well), many people maintain self-diagnosis when they do not need the diagnosis for disability or school or work accommodations—even if they might greatly benefit from a comprehensive and collaborative assessment that validates their experiences and communicates their strengths in meaningful and actionable ways.

Fortunately, with gender, society has largely come over to trusting the expressed authentic experience and communication as the only true indicator of a trans identity, although with children there is still quite a bit of resistance. This case is an example. Despite all the efforts of this school counselor, Amanda's struggles will grow through her teen years if her parents are unable to work with their internalized stigma of Amanda's neurodivergence and trans identity. A supportive community and supportive adults, even if they are unable to effect change with parents, will be key to Amanda's well-being through this time. Parents fearful for their child may default to a position of pushing the child to "toughen up" or "power through" in the hope that this will strengthen their child. The work with these parents is to help them understand that strength comes from honoring oneself and that modeling acceptance and advocacy is the best path forward to helping a child feel strength in who they are. As this commentary has hopefully made clear, the "experts" who parents feel are supporting their child may not be as expert as they hope. These families need all the strength they can muster to center the child's expertise in their experience and identity as we work to create a world that will meet them there.

Expert comment authored by Finn V. Gratton, LMFT, LPCC, San Francisco Bay Area, CA and Benjamin Morsa, PsyD, Berkeley, CA

Take-home messages

More research is needed to determine a link between ASD and gender dysphoria. Some have criticized the existing research that shows a link (dickey and Singh 2020) owing to the way a child is assessed for gender dysphoria using only a single question from the Child Behavior Check List (CBCL) (Achenbach 2001). Given a child needs to be experiencing six of the eight criteria in the *DSM-5* to be diagnosed with gender dysphoria, there is no way a single question could capture all of the diagnostic expectations.

CHAPTER 4

Mixed Parental Support

One very significant challenge a child or adolescent might face is having mixed support from their parents. Whether the child lives with one or both parents can further complicate this situation. It is not uncommon for one parent to pit their child against the other parent when there is a custody battle. In these situations, the parent who is trying to get custody may be upset that the other parent supports the child's gender identity and further may accuse the other parent of being unfit.

Research has shown that trans youth with strong parental support will have better outcomes. The outcomes include better performance in school, quality friend interactions, and reduced mental health concerns (Olson et al. 2016; Ryan et al. 2010). Although it seems like common sense that supporting a person would lead to positive outcomes, this research has been critical in helping parents, guardians, and other caregivers to focus on the needs of the child.

Details of the case

Elijah is an eight-year-old who was assigned male at birth. His mother, Josefina, is of Latina ethnicity and his father, Elgin, is Black. Elijah's parents are married; however, his father is on deployment with the U.S. Army. This is his third deployment. Elijah goes by Elise. Josefina is supportive as long as she restricts dressing up and feminine play to home.

Elgin is much less supportive, and Elise knows when he comes home from his deployment, he will be very angry. This anger will be directed mostly at Josefina. The last time he was home he blamed his wife for "raising a faggot." Elise's parents fight well into the night and Elise is afraid her father will hurt one of them.

One of the neighbors on the army base reports to their command about the constant fighting that comes from Elise's home when Elgin returns from deployment. They are concerned for the safety of Josefina and Elise. Elgin's command is not aware of Elise's gender identity. Although the rules regarding military service are limited to service members, Elgin worries his son's behavior will impact his military career.

Exploring clinical material

Elgin was referred to you, as the psychologist attached to his base. He very reluctantly agreed, mostly because he sensed his commander was on the verge of "writing him up." This is not the first time you have seen Elgin. You saw him after his second deployment. This was true of everyone in his unit, because in addition to losing ten members of their unit when they were shot down, they also lost two soldiers to suicide after returning from the deployment. The command was concerned others in the unit might also be considering suicide.

Elgin was defensive in your first meeting with him. He was adamant that what happens in his home is his business. He states this is why he does not want to live on base. You inquire about the nature of the fights he has with Josefina. Reluctantly he states his wife lets their son act like a girl and that his son is "a pussy."

Psychologist: What do you want for your child?

Elgin: I want him to grow up to be a strong man. My family history is full of men who served our country and were willing to sacrifice their lives for the safety of others.

Psychologist: Serving in the military is an important legacy in your family.

Elgin: It is. I've talked to Josefina about this since we first met. She knows that the Army will not take fags. I can't believe the things she lets him get away with.

Psychologist: Such as?

Elgin: He prances around the house in a dress and Josefina's high heel shoes. His hair is long, and he likes to wear French braids. I just don't understand what she is thinking.

Psychologist: Are you saying that your son is a transgender girl?

Elgin: I'm not sure who or what my son is. I know that what Josefina is doing to him is wrong. God did not make him a girl; he is a boy. Boys do not wear dresses.

In your work with Elgin, it is clear he will "not tolerate" his son's behavior. You refer the family to a counselor in a nearby city as their clinical concerns are not related to your work on the base. This counselor is known to be supportive of trans people and has specialized in family therapy.

General commentary
It may not be surprising that Elgin does not support Elise's behavior, although it could be stereotypical to assume a service member would hold trans-negative attitudes. It can certainly be challenging when one parent is supportive and the other is not. To this point, neither parent has begun to put Elise's well-being at risk. This may not remain the case over time and is an important consideration for your clinical work.

In addition to making a referral to family counseling, it may also be necessary to find a counselor for Elise. Elise, though not yet on the verge of puberty, may be experiencing challenges at school. Chapter 8 of this volume deals with bullying in more detail. Given the climate at home, it is important to understand the difficulties in school and more important is being mindful that your client is Elgin. It is often the case that when a child is having difficulty in school, there are challenges at home. The same could be true about issues at school being influenced by what is happening at home. As Elgin's mental health provider, it is important to help him to understand the ways that interactions with Elise are affecting all parts of her life.

Elgin misses more appointments than he makes. When he shows up, he is guarded in his communication. When he opens up to you, he mostly talks about his anger toward Josefina. You try to explore the stability of their relationship. Elgin says he would never get a divorce. This is due, in part, to there being no family history of divorce. Elgin does not want to be the first to get divorced in his family, but he also does not want his son to be his daughter. He is quite firm about this, and he blames Josefina for his son's behavior.

An affirmative approach to counseling

This case addresses a common situation. One difference in this case from other situations that involve mixed support from parents is that Elise's parents are and intend to remain married. Also different about this case is that the parents have yet to pit their child against one another as one parent attempts to gain control over their child's behavior.

Although Elise is not the client of record, attending to her safety may be important. The case description puts Josefina at risk of violence from Elgin's outbursts of anger. Depending on how Elgin responds to treatment, you may need to ensure Elise's safety. In the event that Elise is at risk of harm, it will be important to make a report to Child Protective Services.

In working with Elgin, it may be helpful to provide him with some basic information about trans people. It is clear Elgin has conflated gender identity with sexual identity (his statement that he does not want his son to be a "faggot"). Elgin may not be aware of the difference between the two concepts. The use of tools such as the *Genderbread Person* (Genderbread Person v 4.0 n.d.) can provide basic education about the difference between sexual and gender identity. Using the most recent version will ensure usage of the correct terminology, which can change rapidly in the trans community. The genderbread person breaks the concepts down to identity (in the brain), attraction (in the heart), expression (in the body and outward appearance), and sex (in biological elements including sex characteristics, hormones, and chromosomes). Elgin may not be open to this type of psychoeducation. Having a copy of the image that you can offer to Elgin will be important. He may be willing to look it over on his own time and then bring questions to a subsequent appointment.

EXPERT COMMENT

Cases like Elise's are not uncommon and must be approached delicately to increase the likelihood of arriving at a positive outcome—one that will result in the child being allowed to flourish and live as their authentic self. First and foremost, when working with youth, it is critical that the providers work thoughtfully to develop strong rapport with the child's parents. It is through this relationship that parents will feel safe expressing their concerns and fears and will be open to learning and growing in their understanding of gender.

In this case, the work with Elise's father is occurring with a separate therapist, but sometimes the child's therapist ends up spending several sessions with one or both parents. Important work in these sessions will likely include helping Elise's father explore his own gender identity development, including the messages he internalized through his own childhood and adolescence about being a boy/man. Helping him understand the gender binary and the way it is damaging to all people—cisgender and transgender—will also be helpful. Additionally, working with Elise's father to understand more about his homophobia will be important. Addressing Elgin's fear for his child and validating this fear will be paramount. Gently and thoughtfully providing psychoeducation to Elgin about gender identity and sexual orientation not being a choice, but instead a part of who they are, will be important. Additionally, emphasizing that, given Elise's age and the limited information Elgin has shared, there is no way to know what Elise's current gender identity is, and equally important, there is no way to predict what her ultimate gender identity and sexual orientation will be is necessary. Because many gender diverse young people ultimately identify as gay or lesbian, it is important to address Elgin's fears about the possible future for Elise as well. Finally, it will be crucial to work with Elgin to help him understand the importance of supporting Elise in her developing sense of gender to prevent significant psychological, emotional, and behavioral problems. Research related to the risks of not doing this should be shared.

In regard to the work with Elise, it would be extremely helpful for her to connect with a therapist who is knowledgeable in working with gender diverse children. This work should include helping Elise explore her gender identity at an appropriate developmental level. Providing psychoeducation around attraction will also be important to help Elise begin to consider more deeply this aspect of her identity. Given that Elise's home has very traditional gender roles, and because of Elise's age, it will be critical to help her understand the gender binary and that we do not have to live within it. It should be explained that at times this means people identify differently than what they were assigned at birth, but this can also mean that being a boy does not have to mean being the breadwinner, joining the military, having a short haircut, or wearing stereotypical male clothing. Children at Elise's age are often still very concrete in their thinking, and depending on their family and broader culture, they may believe that if they enjoy wearing pretty dresses and having long hair it must mean that they are a girl. Providing education to the parents on this topic will be critical as well.

A gender assessment would be useful for Elise, as it would shed more light on some of these factors and could offer specific recommendations for therapy. If it is determined that Elise does identify as a girl, it will be critical to support her in this identity, but simultaneously make sure she understands this does not mean she will always feel this way, and however she identifies at different stages of her life she will be supported. This message will need to be relayed periodically to Elise as she develops and begins to understand her identity and the construct of gender more deeply. It will be important for this message to be relayed to her parents as well, and for all members of the treatment team to fully understand this.

Expert comment authored by Laura Edwards-Leeper, PhD, Hillsboro, OR

Take-home messages

When a child's parents have distinctly different goals for their livelihood, the child, though they may not be at risk of physical harm, will ultimately take the brunt of the conflict. The child is likely to be confused about the mixed messages she receives from her parents. She may understand that her father is not supportive, but she is unlikely to understand why her parents have such different ideas. Elise's parents are in different places with regard to how to provide support. It will be important to validate the feelings of both parents while ensuring they have access to good, reliable information that is supportive of Elise and her exploration of her gender identity.

PART TWO

Adolescence

• CHAPTER 5 •

Puberty, or Why Is My Body Betraying Me?

A rguably, puberty is a difficult time for all adolescents, regardless of their gender identity. Their body has begun changing in ways that may feel out of their control and may not be consistent with their internal sense of gender. This can lead to a host of clinical concerns, some of which will be explored in this chapter. In this chapter I will consider an adolescent who is on the cusp of puberty, has strong family support, and is planning to begin puberty blockers. I explore how to have age-appropriate discussions about parenthood.

It is at the initiation of puberty that a trans adolescent will have the opportunity to access medical treatment. This type of treatment is called gonadotropin releasing hormones (GnRH) or sometimes more commonly, puberty blockers.[2] The use of puberty blockers is explained in more detail in Chapter 10.

Details of the case

María is a 13-year-old who was assigned female at birth. She asserts the use of the name Alejandro and the pronouns he/him/his. Alejandro's parents are David and Angelique. Their family is third-generation Mexican American.

Exploring clinical material

You work in a rural setting and are the only provider who works with adolescents. You have had little training in work with people with diverse gender identities. The nearest provider who works with adolescents and has experience with trans youth is four hours away by car. Though work with trans youth is not your area of expertise, you realize being the only person in town means you sometimes will need to work with clinical concerns that are not quite within your scope of practice.

When you get a call from Angelique asking to see her daughter María you make an appointment for the following week. You have a general idea that María is experiencing some challenges as she approaches puberty. During the intake session Angelique informs you that María has begun acting strange. She has "always been a bit of a tomboy" but that seems to be amplified now. María refuses to wear a purse to keep track of her valuables, she is insistent that she have a short haircut, and she wants to try out for the boys' football team in the fall. María told her mother she knows there are other girls who have played football and she wants to as well.

You ask María to sit in the waiting area while you talk with her mother. The conversation goes like this:

Counselor: Angelique, I appreciate the confidence you have in my work.

Angelique: You are the only person in town who works with teens. I just don't know what to do or where else to go for help. I tried to find someone, but the closest person is over four hours away, and we just don't have the resources to travel that far.

Counselor: I understand your predicament. I asked to speak with you alone because I need for you to understand the limits of my practice.

Angelique: Okay.

Counselor: I have worked with adolescents most of my career. I'm not concerned about that aspect of working with María. I don't have experience working with transgender people. I have taken a one-hour workshop on the topic, but that doesn't make me qualified to work with María.

Angelique: What am I going to do?

Counselor: Before you lose hope about this, let me share the ideas I have about how I can be supportive in this work. When I attended the workshop, I got the name and email address of the speaker. I was really impressed with their knowledge and the ways they related to adolescents. I would like to reach out to this person and see if they would be willing, or know someone else who would be willing, to consult with me about María. I would not use any identifying information when I talk to my colleagues.

Angelique: What do you mean by identifying information?

Counselor: I won't tell this person María's name, the town she lives in, her age, things like that. I do that when I consult with others so they might learn enough about my client without being able to identify who they are. Plus, this person lives in California, so it's unlikely they would figure it out. How does that sound?

Angelique: That sounds fine.

Counselor: Let's invite María back into the room. [María returns.] Thanks for your patience María. I wanted to talk with your mom about some of the challenges I have in working with you. I think we figured out a good solution.

María: Okay.

After María and Angelique leave your office, you find the information you brought home from the workshops on working with transgender people. You get in touch with Dr. Luke Jamison. Dr. Jamison is unable to work with you at this time, but he recommends you get in touch with a professional colleague named Eliz Meyer. Luke explains that Eliz worked under his supervision and has recently begun providing consultation services. Luke thinks your case is just the type of work Eliz will enjoy and be helpful with.

You reach out to Eliz, and they (Eliz uses the non-binary pronouns they/them/their) agree to work with you. You learn that they are the provider who is about four hours away from your location. You ask Eliz for resources and they provide you with a list of books and articles they have found to be helpful over the years (see the list of supplemental materials in the Further Reading and Other Resources section).

You thank Eliz and tell them that you will be in touch again after you have met again with the client.

María and Angelique return the next week. You are happy to let them know you found a consultation resource and that it is the person who works four hours away. You all chuckle about that coincidence.

You meet with María alone moving forward. María's mother is always available in the lobby should you need her input. María first states firmly that she wants to be called Alejandro and asks that you use male pronouns (he/him/his). You frequently make mistakes with both the name and the pronouns. You try to catch yourself and apologize, but you do not always do so. At the beginning of the next session, Alejandro's mother asks to speak with you first and you agree. Angelique tells you that Alejandro is upset with you because you keep using the wrong name or pronoun. You apologize for this and have some trouble not getting defensive. Reluctantly, Alejandro agrees to see you that day. Alejandro does not say much and answers your questions with short, curt answers. At the end of the session, you again apologize to Alejandro and his mother. You go on at some length about how hard this has been for you and promise to get in touch with Eliz.

When you reach Eliz, you explain the situation. They note that you have never made a mistake with their name or pronouns and wonder why this is so hard with Alejandro. You say that the biggest reason why it is hard is because you first knew Alejandro as María. You admit you have always had a hard time when someone you know gets married and takes a new last name. You equate these as similar situations. In your conversation with Eliz, you are reminded that trans people find it disrespectful when people do not use their affirmed name or pronouns. The simple act of admitting your mistake takes the pressure off of the trans person to correct you. And, it can be especially hard for a client to correct their provider due to the power imbalance that favors the provider. Hearing it this way helps you to make more sense out of why this was so hard for Alejandro. You make a note to be sure that your apology is never lengthier than the mistake.

Puberty blockers and their impact

Alejandro has been talking with his parents about when he might be able to begin puberty blockers. He has not started puberty, but he admits he is scared of how his body will change. He especially loves having a flat chest and states that his older sisters both have large chests and that would be the worst thing for him. You feel it is important that both the parents and Alejandro be present for this discussion. After some effort, you are able to find a time for the session. David's work schedule is very demanding. You begin the session by asking Alejandro to share with his parents his fears about starting puberty. The two of you have been practicing this conversation. Alejandro talks to his parents about what it would mean for him if his body went through puberty. His parents are attentive and ask appropriate questions such as the risks and benefits of blocking puberty. They also ask about how to find a medical provider who would prescribe this medicine. You hand Angelique a list of four providers. None are nearby, but all are reported to have a good reputation in this area. You also offer to write a letter of introduction to the prescribing provider (see sample letters in Appendix B).

Since no one has brought it up yet, you broach the topic of parenting. You ask Alejandro if he has given any thought to whether or not he would like to be a parent someday. He has not really thought about this and is wondering why you brought it up. You mention that Alejandro may need to think about whether he wants to be a biological parent. Each family member has a quizzical look on their face. You go on to say that blocking puberty may have unintended consequences. In general, puberty blockers stop most of what happens during puberty. This includes the maturation process of eggs in people assigned female at birth (AFAB) and sperm in people assigned male at birth (AMAB). If these cells never grow to maturity, a person will not be able to get pregnant or get someone else pregnant. Alejandro admits he has never thought about that. Alejandro and his parents agree that they will talk about this at home.

Whether Alejandro decides he wants to be a parent or not, it may be necessary to revisit this conversation, as his decision about parenting may change. In those upcoming conversations you can talk with Alejandro about the technologies that exist to preserve eggs, sperm, and fertilized eggs. You can also talk about the options around adoption and becoming a foster parent. Prior to having those conversations, it is important that you make your best effort to learn about the adoption and foster laws in your states. Some states have favorable laws while others do not.

Having these conversations at an age-appropriate level, or letting the parents lead the discussion, is important. There are different views on when a child should learn about sex and related topics. Although this can be a highly charged topic depending on a person's values, if an adolescent is to start puberty blockers, they need to understand all of the risks and benefits. Not being able to provide genetic material (e.g., egg or sperm) is a potential risk.

EXPERT COMMENT

Thirteen-year-old Alejandro (AFAB) comes to establish a therapeutic relationship with the ultimate goal of beginning gender-affirming care. Other stated or inferred goals include the use of the name Alejandro instead of the assigned name María, the use of male pronouns, obtaining a puberty blocker, and the avoidance of the development of female breasts.

Potential challenges include the rural nature of the practice, the lack of area healthcare providers who are experienced in transgender care, and a possible cultural mismatch in working with a third-generation Mexican American family.

The therapist is open about having had little experience in dealing with transgender youth and arranges an appropriate consultative relationship with another provider. The therapist is in an awkward position: being honest about their lack of experience but willing to find a work-around. It would have been reasonable for the therapist to have declined service, but certainly less optimal for the patient. Twenty years ago, my first transgender patient asked if I would take care of her, and I declined. Having had no training in transgender medicine, I thought it almost *responsible* to decline. By the time another trans woman asked for care, I was ready to shoulder my discomfort to better serve the client.

I would like to have known more about Alejandro's exploration of gender. In my experience, it's a directed and informed 13-year-old who knows about puberty blockers at all. I would not be surprised if Alejandro knew all about chest binders and top surgery.

With respect to the puberty blocker, I feel quite safe discussing this with a patient and their family. The puberty blocker simply puts puberty on "pause," giving everyone a chance to catch their breath and figure out what to do next. When a blocker implant is removed, puberty will resume, chugging along in the way it was genetically programmed to do. Reproductive capacity should then be intact—unless the patient begins cross-sex hormones—in which case Alejandro may not have developed far enough into puberty to allow for mature eggs. That said, on occasion trans men who start transitioning after puberty have stopped testosterone and planned and carried a pregnancy using sperm from a partner or sperm donor.

Most healthcare providers misgender a client accidentally and on rare occasions. Even trans people may misgender themselves or each other. To a trans youth, misgendering is a microaggression—painful and insulting. There's no getting the foot out of the mouth at that point; apologize sincerely and move on. Say something like, "I'm terribly sorry, Alejandro. I do appreciate you speaking up for yourself." And then, do not do it again!

As healthcare providers, we find ourselves in uncomfortable positions from time to time. We would like to be all-knowing and at ease with every situation—but we simply are not. Responsible, caring providers do live with a certain amount of discomfort in the name of delivering good care. It was fortunate that Alejandro had a therapist who was willing to shoulder some discomfort for the patient's benefit.

Expert comment authored by Linda Gromko, MD, Seattle, WA

Take-home messages

Be willing to admit your mistakes. Names and pronouns are very individual and also very important. Your client may not feel safe in correcting you. When you admit your mistake, though it does not correct the mistake, your client may feel safer as you work together.

Have age-appropriate conversations. In the example in this chapter, the counselor begins a discussion about parenting without having talked to anyone in the family about the idea. It is understandable that each of the family members was confused about the discussion. Minimally, it will be important to talk with Alejandro and his parents, perhaps in separate conversations, before the discussion with the full family.

CHAPTER 6

Co-occurring Concerns in Adolescence: Cutting and Suicidality

M ental health providers hope their clients will not attempt or die by suicide. Similarly, having a client who engages in self-injury can be challenging. In both situations, helping the client to build prosocial coping skills is the most prudent clinical course, ensuring of course that the client is safe.

Suicide and self-injury are far too common for trans people. Research indicates 40 percent or more of trans people have either attempted suicide at least once and/or engaged in nonsuicidal self-injury (dickey, Reisner, and Juntunen 2015; James et al. 2016). dickey and Budge (2020) address the rates of suicide as a public health crisis. The problem is, no one is actively working to develop interventions that address suicide and self-injury as a clinical concern for trans people.

In this chapter, I explore the ways cutting and suicidal thinking impact a trans adolescent. Critical to work with anyone who has a history of suicide and nonsuicidal self-injury (NSSI) is the need to help the adolescent develop skills to counter emotional dysregulation.

Details of the case
Madison is a 15-year-old who was assigned female at birth. Madison wavers between a masculine and a non-binary identity. Madison uses they/them/their pronouns. You have been seeing Madison for about

one year. They first came to see you because their parents were concerned about their safety. Madison reports having attempted suicide more than 15 times and having been hospitalized five times. Madison has dropped out of school. They move between their parent's homes because they are divorced. Madison reports they get more support at their father's house than at their mother's. Madison states that their mother comes from a religiously conservative family and the family wants nothing to do with Madison. Although Madison's father is more supportive, he does not understand his "daughter," especially "her" tendency to engage in self-injury and attempt suicide. The last time Madison attempted suicide they were hospitalized for several weeks.

In your work with Madison, you attempt to build coping skills such as mindfulness and distress tolerance. You would like for Madison to participate in Dialectical Behavior Therapy (DBT) (Linehan 2015b; Pederson and Pederson 2017); however, the nearest group is over one hundred miles away. Madison can, at times, be reluctant to work with you even though they show up for sessions.

Exploring clinical material

Madison was recently discharged from the hospital after engaging in self-injury that required medical attention. This is not the first time that Madison has cut themselves in such a way that required medical attention. The most recent time was different from the others. Madison deliberately chose a time to engage in cutting when they knew their father would be away from home for several hours. By the time he returned home, Madison had lost a significant amount of blood. They were rushed to the hospital and after they were stabilized they were placed in the in-patient psychiatric unit. In your experience with Madison, they learn new skills and feel better after having been hospitalized, but they return to poor coping skills (e.g., drugs, alcohol, sexual behavior).

Madison first identified as non-binary at the age of 13. They feel certain they are trans but have not been able to decide between a masculine or non-binary identity. Madison came to see you last year after they were expelled from school for chronic truancy, drug behavior on campus, and failing grades. You are aware the local high school will expel students for poor grades as the school is concerned about the overall ratings of student academic success. Initially, Madison's father agreed to home school them, but that fell by the wayside and Madison spends most of their time surfing the internet, listening to music, and drawing. Consider the following conversation with Madison after they have been discharged from the hospital.

Psychologist: Hi Madison, it is nice to see you again.

Madison: Hello.

Psychologist: I know you were just discharged from the hospital. How did things go for you there?

Madison: Same shit, different day—you know that.

Psychologist: You seem angrier than normal. Did something happen in the hospital?

Madison: Just the usual. I went to group every day and saw a counselor every other day. The psychiatrist saw me during the week, but not on the weekends. I guess it was okay. I just wish things would get less difficult for me.

Psychologist: Less difficult how?

Madison: For starters, I hate having a period. It's a constant reminder that my body and my mind are in two different places.

Psychologist: We've talked about that before. I remember how distressing that is for you. Do you remember the skills we worked on to help you cope with that?

Madison: Not really.

Psychologist: We worked on the STOP skills for the times when you feel as though you are in crisis mode…

Your work with Madison is both rewarding and challenging. You have developed a good clinical relationship with Madison, and you look forward to your sessions with them. Much of your work has focused on developing DBT skills such as STOP. STOP stands for: stop, take a step back, observe, and proceed mindfully (Linehan 2015a). You know there is little you can do to change Madison's living condition.

To this point, Madison has not divulged anything that would lead you to suspect abuse in the home. You understand some of their distress as being related to Madison's minimal contact with their peer group. The benefit to that is they are no longer experiencing bullying in school. However, their interactions with other people are limited to their immediate family members. To ensure Madison is supervised, they often accompany one of their parents at work.

General commentary

Parts of Madison's story are far from uncommon in the trans and non-binary communities. Research has shown that 42 percent of trans adults reported a history of self-injury (dickey et al. 2015). Additionally, multiple studies have shown that 40 percent of trans adults of reported a history of attempting suicide at least once (Grant et al. 2011; James et al. 2016). These numbers are alarming and represent a public health crisis (dickey and Budge 2020). The mental health needs of trans and non-binary people, regardless of their age, must be taken seriously without unnecessarily pathologizing their experience.

Much has been written about trans people and social determinants of health (SDOH) (Blosnich et al. 2017; dickey, Budge, Katz-Wise, and Garza 2016; Dysart-Gale 2010; Hatzenbuehler and Pachankis 2016; Pega and Veale 2015). We also know that, in general, when a person experiences sub-optimal SDOH they are more likely to have diminished resources as it relates to addressing basic needs. For example, as we think about Madison, in additional to experiences of self-injury and attempted suicide, they are also missing important developmental milestones. Madison has been out of school for over a year with no plan to re-engage. Missing educational experiences and the social learning that takes place in the school environment places Madison at risk for homelessness and the sequelae. This may include becoming involved in the sex and drug trade as a means of obtaining income, a place to stay, or a meal.

An affirmative approach to counseling

Working with Madison to help ensure they are able to access coping skills is a starting place. Moving beyond that, it will be important to help Madison understand their resilience (Singh 2013). Resilience is defined as one's ability to bounce back from diversity (Singh, Hays, and Watson 2011). In helping Madison see their ability to tolerate emotional dysregulation without hurting themselves, you can hope they will be able to build those skills, so they become automatic.

Another way to think about working with trans and non-binary youth who have a history of self-injury and suicide attempts is to help them understand how their life maps onto Maslow's hierarchy of needs (Maslow 1943). Explain to them that when they are working to meet their safety needs, they are unlikely to have the energy to focus on belonging needs and so on. Even though Maslow's work was first published many years ago, the concepts still fit. It is possible to see self-actualization as related to making a gender transition. If a trans person is never able to fully meet their more basic needs, it might be hard for them to make a successful transition.

In understanding the needs of trans and non-binary adolescents with a history of self-injury or suicidal behavior, one must be careful to address the other intersecting identities the adolescent possesses. This is addressed more fully in Chapter 13, but with adolescents it is important to keep in mind that some of their intersecting identities may not be fully developed. Being ready to help your clients explore how those identities impact their life will be important (Chang et al. 2018).

Theoretical approaches to understanding suicide in transgender people

Two theoretical concepts are used to explain suicide by trans people. These are minority stress theory (MST) (Meyer 1995, 2003) and demoralization (Woodrum 2019). MST was first applied to sexual minorities and the ways that challenges they encounter complicate life experiences. MST has been applied to the lives of trans people as well (Goldblum et al. 2012; Hendricks and Testa 2012; Tebbe and Moradi 2016). MST proposes that distal and proximal stressors, in addition to the anticipation of stressors, put trans people at higher risk for suicide. Demoralization, or the deep sense that a person is helpless, hopeless, and meaningless, has been associated with risk of suicide (Woodrum 2019). Although demoralization and MST have not been applied to

NSSI in trans people, given the connection in suicidal behavior and thinking, it is possible that they both have a connection with NSSI.

EXPERT COMMENT

Madison is a strong example of the struggle with suicide and self-injury trans masculine and non-binary adolescents can face, highlighting critical elements that clinicians will want to address as part of treatment. Research continues to find that, within the trans population, those assigned female at birth and non-binary individuals report the highest rates of suicide attempts and self-injury (Grossman, Park, and Russell 2016; Toomey, Syvertsen, and Shramko 2018). Some of this elevated risk among trans masculine and non-binary adolescents could be due to the intersecting challenges of body dissatisfaction and identity struggles, both of which are seen in Madison's case. Regarding the body, Madison expresses intense anger at continuing to experience their period, which acts as a constant reminder their body is not matching their sense of self. A handful of studies have noted that self-injury is motivated by strong dissatisfaction with and disregard for the body (dickey, Reisner, and Juntunen 2015; Muehlenkamp 2012; Peterson et al. 2017). In their sample of trans and non-binary persons, Morris and Galupo (2019) reported that NSSI was used primarily to manage and reduce gender dysphoria by distracting oneself from one's body dissatisfaction and/or social disapproval of one's gender identity or appearance. Furthermore, there is some evidence self-injury may decrease following transition (Davey, Arcelus, Meyer, and Bouman 2015), indicating the potential importance of body–gender matching. Clinical interventions that encourage and support gender-congruent expression, body-esteem building, and exploration of transition options may therefore help to reduce self-injury (Owen-Smith et al. 2018).

At the same time, it is equally important to recognize the discrimination and social rejection individuals face for nonconforming gender expression (Herman, Haas, and Rodgers 2014; Reisner et al. 2015), which Madison faced at school through bullying and within their maternal family. Clinicians need to simultaneously teach adaptive coping skills for managing the strong emotions arising from such rejecting and discriminatory experiences, much like the DBT skills being taught to Madison, while validating the legitimacy of the emotions. Madison is also unsure if a masculine or non-binary identity best fits their sense of self. A key developmental task of adolescence is to solidify one's sense of self. When the identity development process is disrupted, especially due to societal and/or familial disapproval, the adolescent may internalize the negative views contributing to trans-negativity, low self-esteem, and self-hate (Marshall et al. 2016; Rood et al. 2017), all of which are known risk factors for suicide. In Madison's case we see they feel unsupported by family and are socially isolated having dropped out of school and spending most of their time online or engaging in risky behaviors. Helping Madison use social media/the internet for support, to engage with positive trans role models and other trans or non-binary youth, may help protect against further suicide attempts (Johns et al. 2018). Sharing trans-specific crisis resources such as The Trevor Project and online community support groups aligns with gender-affirming treatment approaches (Puckett et al. 2018) and may strengthen a sense of belonging while providing identity validation and thereby decreasing suicide risk. Treatment approaches that utilize a functional analysis, where the factors that precipitate and maintain problem behaviors are explored (Linehan 2015b; Pederson and Pederson 2017), are recommended as they identify places to target for coping skill development and/or problem solving.

Overall, Madison's case highlights how suicide and self-injury are multidetermined behaviors with various contextual and internal factors intersecting to elevate risk. As such, it is imperative clinicians working with trans youth inquire regularly about suicide and monitor self-injury throughout care. Treatments focusing on affect regulation, adaptive coping, and family support are supported strategies for reducing NSSI (Klonsky et al. 2011). Finding ways to include family and provide formal support so families can understand, cope with, and support their child is critical to reducing suicide risk with trans youth (Oransky, Burke, and Steever 2019). Given the social isolation/rejection and internalized trans negativity often experienced by trans youth, group interventions are also recommended to build a sense of belonging (a key protective factor for suicide), decrease self-stigma, and assist with positive identity development (Corrigan, Kosyluk, and Rüsch 2013; Marshall et al. 2016; Yanos, Roe, and Lysaker 2011). Incorporating body-esteem and gender expression as key elements within gender-affirming treatment approaches (dickey and Budge 2020; Puckett et al. 2018) is likely to enhance the effectiveness of treatment for reducing self-injury and suicidal behaviors. Multi-level approaches to therapy that address the individual, relational, environmental, and societal factors contributing to, and protecting against, suicide risk and self-injury are required to truly decrease rates of suicide among trans and non-binary youth (Puckett 2019) like Madison.

Expert comment authored by Jennifer J. Muehlenkamp, PhD, Eau Claire, WI

Take-home messages

This case brings to light a common and disturbing trend seen in the lives of trans people. That is, trans people are at elevated risk for suicide and self-injury. There is a need to ensure your comfort with querying about a client's safety. Equally important is the ability to identify risk and protective factors that can be used to develop a safety plan for your clients. For providers in training, comfort with asking about suicide and self-injury takes practice. If you are having trouble with this skill, please seek out supervision. Your supervisor does not expect you to have this all figured out. Asking deeply personal and difficult questions takes practice. Your supervisor will be able to help you work through your reluctance and any awkwardness.

Given the high rates of suicide attempts and self-injury in trans and non-binary communities, supervisors are encouraged to ensure their own level of competence with this client group. It is not acceptable for mental health providers to expect their trans and non-binary clients to educate them about trans experiences. Similarly, a trainee should not be expected to train their supervisors. It is unacceptable for a trainee to stop consulting with their supervisor about work with their trans clients because the supervisor overly pathologizes the client's history or uses outdated and harmful conceptualizations.

CHAPTER 7

Non-Binary Identities

Trans people have existed throughout history. Indigenous peoples throughout the world had what would today be considered non-binary identities. To be clear, what is similar is that many people from Indigenous cultures held to an identity that was not consistent with the sex they were assigned at birth, nor was it consistent with the gender binary.

Although people with non-binary identities have existed throughout history, there has been an increase in the number of people who are claiming non-binary identities. Non-binary individuals may not identify as transgender, in the same way that many transgender people do not identify as transsexual. Generally speaking, people have some difficulty embracing people with non-binary identities. This is due, in part, to the many ways that the gender binary is reinforced across many aspects of life, including attire, hair style, education, career choices, medical care, gender roles, and communication styles. Consider the following case.

Details of the case

Royal is a 16-year-old who was assigned male at birth. Royal has a non-binary identity and is African American. They were given the name Antonne at birth and have been using the name Royal for the past three years. Royal uses they/them/their pronouns. Royal is a junior in high school. They first came to see you when they began exploring their gender identity. Royal has mixed support from their parents. More often than not, their parents use the wrong name and they never use the correct pronouns. This is frustrating for Royal. They report that their friend group and others at school are supportive. Royal recently started a Gender and Sexuality Alliance (GSA[3]) at their school.

Royal would like to block testosterone. They would eventually like to have an orchiectomy (removal of their testes). At this time, they are having difficulty finding a medical provider who will start them on an androgen blocker. This is due, in part, to Royal's parents' unwillingness to consent to this treatment. In the meantime, Royal is becoming distressed as they develop secondary sex characteristics.

Exploring clinical material

Working with Royal should not be terribly complicated, unless you are unable to work with their parents to gain their permission (consent) for medical treatment. By the time a person reaches adolescence, they are pretty sure they know what is right. This is especially true when considering the expectations of one's parents. Royal has spent many hours researching the various medical treatments available to trans people. Although they have a non-binary identity, they would like to have this one surgery as they feel "repulsed" by the ways that testosterone makes them feel.

As you work with Royal it becomes clear that their parents will not consent to treatment. Your work will need to shift so you can help Royal develop prosocial coping skills. To this point, Royal has denied being a danger to themselves. This includes thoughts of ending their life and self-injury. Still, you are significantly concerned for Royal's well-being. Even though you have been working with Royal on coping skills, they seem more and more depressed each time they come to your office.

Psychologist: Hi Royal.

Royal: Hey, how are you?

Psychologist: I'm fine. More importantly, how are you doing?

Royal: Okay, I guess.

Psychologist: What does that mean, okay?

Royal: It feels like I will never be able to be my real self. I sort of get where my parents are coming from, but I wish they would just let me do this. Waiting until I turn 18 feels like forever from now.

And what is it about being 18 that suddenly I can make whatever decisions I want to?

Psychologist: This is the hard part that we talked about. Right now, you feel helpless to take actions that are about your body and your life...

Royal: When I get really down, I think about running away.

Psychologist: Where would you go?

Royal: I don't really know. I've been talking to a friend online who lives in San Francisco. He says I can crash with him. He also says he knows other trans youth he can introduce me to.

Psychologist: Would you really leave your family behind? [At this point, you are concerned Royal is going to follow through on their plan to run away. You have talked about the kinds of information you would need to report to Royal's parents. This falls into a gray area.]

Royal seems willing to engage in safety planning and says they only think about running away when they are feeling very desperate. You work with Royal to help them engage with the others in their school who are supportive: members of the GSA. You also, with Royal's permission, reach out to the GSA advisor to ask about how things are going with the organization. You learn that even though Royal started the group, they have not been attending recently. You ask whether it would be helpful to come to one of the groups to talk about some of the challenges that arise when a person is in puberty. You also want to provide the members of the GSA with some skills around supporting themselves and one another.

One of the students suggests that maybe they could have a buddy system. They talk about last year at summer camp. Whenever they went on a hike, they had a buddy who would look out for them and vice versa. The students quickly buddy up and make room for a trio. The students engage in some brainstorming and decide that the following guidelines will apply:

- Each student will reach out to their buddy when they are having a rough time.

- The buddy will respond to the message by providing support.

- If one of the buddies does not hear from the other by an agreed-upon time, they will reach out to the buddy to be sure they are safe.

- Buddies will use provided local suicide prevention resources in the event their emotional state elevates to a crisis.

- Buddies have their buddy's permission to reach out to a parent if they are concerned for their buddy's safety.

General commentary

Simply being aware of the risks for suicide and self-injury is not enough to ensure the safety of our clients. It is, however, an important starting place. Trans youth are likely dealing with a number of concerns that may be complicated by their gender identity. Puberty is a difficult time for most people.

To this point in the book we have only talked briefly about the importance of social support. Trans people can struggle on multiple levels related to social support. First is the feeling that they are alone in their questions about their gender. This is becoming less of a concern as the internet continues to grow. Youth; people who live in rural settings; and those who live in religiously, politically, and socially conservative areas are likely to feel isolated. Similar to how people can connect on the internet as mentioned above, there are numerous web sites that address all manner of social connections. Parents are cautioned, however, to pay attention to their child's internet behaviors. Not all sites are safe for minors and some are unsafe even for adults. Another aspect of social isolation can relate to intimate relationships. If a trans person is in an abusive relationship, they may be socially isolated (Burnes et al. 2016; Richmond, Burnes, and Carroll 2012; Richmond, Burnes, Singh, and Ferrara 2017). This is a very difficult type of intimate partner violence (IPV) (Cronholm et al. 2011; Reuter et al. 2017; Walker 2015). Finally, some trans people will have difficulty asking for support in the times when they need it most. Encouraging participation in online or in-person support groups can help to alleviate the isolation (dickey and Loewy 2010; Heck 2017).

An affirmative approach to counseling

Trans adolescents should be able to initiate puberty blockers (e.g., gonadotropin releasing hormones or GnRH treatment). The initiation of puberty blockers is not without controversy. This treatment was originally used to arrest precocious puberty. The thinking was that the child interacts with peers more successfully if they are experiencing an age-concordant puberty. When using puberty blockers with trans adolescents, it is important to initiate treatment as the adolescent begins puberty. This is also known as Tanner Stage 2 of development. Everyone is in Tanner Stage 1 from birth until puberty commences. If a trans person has to go through an endogenous puberty, they are likely to be distressed with the development of secondary sex characteristics that are consistent with the sex they were assigned at birth. When you are able to block puberty, the adolescent will not have an endogenous physical developmental experience.

The implications of starting puberty blockers may have unintended consequences. Because puberty has been blocked, the adolescent may not develop mature gametes. This means that they may not have the ability to provide genetic material for procreation (e.g., eggs or sperm). It may be important to have an age-appropriate discussion with the adolescent about their hopes and plans for parenthood. It is possible that the adolescent has not fully considered this, but they need to know the implications of the treatment (see Chapter 5 for additional material on puberty blockers and parenting decisions). It is relatively simple to cryopreserve sperm, but the same is not true for an unfertilized egg. Unfertilized eggs are quite fragile and more difficult to preserve (dickey, Ducheny, and Ehrbar 2016). Some questions to consider:

- If an adolescent wants to preserve their eggs and ensure they will remain viable at a later time, whose sperm would be used to fertilize the eggs?

- If an adolescent wants to initiate puberty for the purpose of obtaining mature gametes, do they have the skills to manage the challenges associated with an endogenous puberty?

- If an adolescent AFAB decides to harvest their gametes after commencing puberty, are they aware of the possible need for large doses of hormones to harvest eggs?

As this can be a difficult conversation, it may be important to have the discussion with the adolescent and possibly also their parent. Adolescents may not be ready to make such a decision about their future. Additionally, their parents may not want you to be the one who leads those conversations.

Another aspect of supporting non-binary adolescents is the importance of honoring, even celebrating, their identity. Although young people tend to be more flexible in thinking about gender and sexuality, this is not ubiquitous. This is one of the reasons why youth often face mistreatment from their peers. When working with an adolescent, you may need to ask more than once about how things are going at school. The adolescent may initially say that everything is fine. However, you are likely to learn more about the ways they are having to stand up for themselves if you ask more specific questions about school. For example, instead of asking "How are things at school?" you might instead say "I know that we talked about some challenging interactions you have been having at school. Tell me how that is going now." The client may not be more forthcoming, but by foregrounding previous concerns, your client may feel safer to talk about what is really going on.

EXPERT COMMENT

This chapter presents a range of important considerations for people who work with transgender and non-binary youth. The chapter begins by highlighting Indigenous cultural conceptualizations of gender as being different than those of the modern Western world. It is essential not to reduce Indigenous cultures to a monolith and not to appropriate aspects of a culture without context. Instead, there is a need to reframe discussion of gender by noting that gender is relative to the culture in which it exists; this framework helps us critically interrogate the medicalization of trans and non-binary identities in Western culture. Gender dysphoria (American Psychiatric Association 2013) is conceptualized as a mental health condition, and gender-affirming interventions, such as hormone therapy, are the treatment for this condition. Medical interventions for trans people were not designed for non-binary people, nor do they support a deconstruction of Western concepts of binary gender. Instead, medicalized transition can feel like a further reification of the man/woman binary, and non-binary people can struggle to fit into this paradigm.

Being critical of how culture treats medical transition does not diminish the need for access to medical care for trans and non-binary youth. Instead, this kind of reflection is crucial for understanding the myriad factors that interplay for non-binary youth when understanding their identities. Compared to binary trans identities, there are fewer narratives about non-binary identities that youth can use as a guide. As a result, youth may need more support in plotting their own gender path and exploring the variety of options available. As highlighted in this chapter, medical transition can present a range of options for non-binary youth. Some non-binary youth may have no interest in medical transition; some non-binary youth may want access to medical care that may not fall into traditional gender-affirming care. Other youth may feel conflicted about which steps to take and be worried about the reactions of others. Some youth may feel pressured toward medical transition to validate their non-binary identity, while other youth may feel very confident in wanting a medical transition, but struggle to explain to others their non-binary identities when seeking a more traditional medical transition. Clinicians working with non-binary youth need to be able to hold all of these possibilities, and more, as they support youth in better understanding their identities.

Beyond supporting youth, clinicians working with trans and non-binary youth must be able to help the family. This chapter only briefly touches on Royal's family, but it is essential to gain a deeper understanding of the barriers to support. Clinicians need to move past the dichotomous thinking about parental support (e.g., supportive versus non-supportive) and instead fully evaluate the family system. What are the reasons that Royal's family does not want to support medical interventions? Do they need time to adjust to the idea, do they need more information, are they avoiding the decision out of anxiety? Even if their parents will not support a medical transition, are there other ways for the family to be supportive? Would practicing pronouns in session be helpful? Would books or connections to other families with non-binary youth help? Families hold a great deal of power when working with non-binary youth and the more that a clinician can support families, the more they ultimately support youth.

Expert comment authored by Kinton Rossman, PhD
and Addis Green, BA, both of Chicago, IL

Take-home messages

Trans adolescents with non-binary identities are becoming more common. Some might even say that telling others they have a trans or non-binary identity can have a social contagion effect in a school (Wadman 2018). There is no validated evidence that this is actually a reality. This is true as well of so-called "rapid onset gender dysphoria" (ROGD). What appears to be ROGD may simply be that the adolescent has finally come out to their family, and the family feels like treatment is moving very quickly (Wadman 2018).

ROGD was first suggested by Littman (2018). In her work, she explored the experiences of parents as their children came out with a trans identity. Littman found there was a large group of trans children who were AFAB. Littman called this an inversion, as previously one would see more children and adolescents who were assigned male at birth having a trans identity. Littman's work has been criticized by scholars and trans activists (Ashley and Baril 2018). Ashley and Baril characterize ROGD as young people having been "misled into claiming a trans identity before they truly understand what that means" (p.1). Peers, social media, and popular media are all implicated in having influenced the child to claim a trans identity. Key to the concept of ROGD is that the young person does not have a history of questioning their gender prior to puberty. Marchiano (2017) likens ROGD to suicide and eating disorder clusters. Marchiano also reports being disturbed at learning that some trans masculine individuals had chest masculinization surgery at the age of 14. Marchiano mistakenly likens the initiation of hormone therapy to "permanent sterilization." I talked earlier about how puberty blockers can have this effect. What I failed to state is that if puberty blocking treatment is halted, the adolescent will resume with an endogenous puberty. An orchiectomy and a hysterectomy are the two permanent surgical procedures that a trans person may undergo that are irreversible treatments that will result in sterilization.

Marchiano (2017) correctly suggests that all people, regardless of their gender or gender identity, should be able to express their gender and participate in activities in whatever way feels most salient for them. Complicated in the discussion of ROGD are the reports that most children do not persist in their gender identity. In the research literature, these children are known as desisters. The research that identifies high rates of desistance is flawed in that it assumes that if a child did not follow up with treatment then they were not trans (Temple-Newhook et al. 2018). This does not take into account the fact that the child and their family may have moved elsewhere, sought treatment from a new provider, or are simply waiting until they reach the age of majority in their country. Marchiano reports on people who have "detransitioned." One of the aspects of transition that may not be addressed is that it is hard to know if a person will be satisfied with the results of a medical transition. Unlike many other things a person might do in their life, some aspects of a medical transition are permanent. This may be an area where people with non-binary identities who choose not to engage in a medical transition have an advantage. If they have not made a medical transition there is no need to detransition physically, only socially. I do not mean to minimize the social and emotional cost of detransitioning. This can be a challenge whether a person has made a medical, social, or legal transition. However, if a person has completed one or more medical interventions, these may not be reversible. As Rossman and Green suggest, people with non-binary identities may choose to transition in a variety of ways, which may include medical interventions. Although historically speaking there was a narrative about "how to be trans," this is no longer the case and most reputable mental health providers understand that transition will look different from one person to the next.

CHAPTER 8

Bullying

Although we have waited until the adolescent section to discuss bullying, this can begin in childhood. Bullying has existed for many years and often happens because an adolescent behaves and presents themselves in a way that is inconsistent with gender norms. Regardless of the reason why a person experiences bullying, it is fair to say that those experiences can have a lasting and significant impact on the person's self-esteem.

Bullying is defined as "written, verbal, or physical conduct, including via electronic communication, that is sufficiently severe, persistent, or pervasive to limit a student's ability to participate in, or benefit from, a program or activity" (GLSEN and NCTE 2018, p.2). Bullying may be a single incident or a series of events that target a particular person or group of people. Regardless of the reasons behind the bullying, schools and other institutions must have a zero-tolerance policy for this behavior without being punitive and authoritarian (Gregory, Cornell, Fan, and Sheras 2010). One of the challenges for the person who is bullied is that they do not often see the punishment faced by the person who engaged in bullying because there may be privacy concerns that prevent administrators from making that information public. This can be especially difficult as it may feel as though nothing was done to protect the victim.

Details of the case

Abe is a 12-year-old Alaska Native in the seventh grade. Abe is enrolled in the Inuit nation. Abe was assigned female at birth and though they have a masculine presentation, they identify as two-spirit. Abe uses the gender-neutral pronouns they/them/their. Abe's family and tribal leadership are supportive of Abe's identity.

Exploring clinical material

Abe was a good student through the sixth grade. Abe was especially good in math and science classes. Because of that, they were selected to participate in a two-week science, technology, engineering, and math (STEM) summer program at the University of Washington. When Abe returned home from the two-week program they were very excited to apply what they had learned. Abe made time over the rest of the summer to explore their ideas about medicine. This included spending time with the *angakkuq* (medicine man or shaman) of their tribe. The result of this experience was that the *angakkuq* (Edward) decided to take Abe under his wing to begin to teach them about the ways of the tribe with regard to health and spiritual concerns. Abe and Edward met once or twice a week for up to three hours. Abe's parents were very excited about their interest.

This excitement ebbed partway through the fall of seventh grade. Abe's parents, Melissa and Joseph, learned that Abe was failing most of their classes when they had a parent–teacher conference. Melissa and Joseph were initially concerned that this was the first they had heard of Abe having struggles at school. The teacher shared that she was not sure when or how the problems began. She had been looking forward to having Abe in her class this year. She had heard many good things about Abe's academic abilities and was excited to see where that would go this year.

You receive a call from Melissa. She is distraught about Abe's situation, and she does not know who else to reach out to. You live hundreds of miles away and Abe's family lives in a very remote part of Alaska. There are no roads to their town, and you can only access the town by air. You have recently begun to see people using a secure telehealth portal. Melissa reports that they do not have internet at home and do not know how they might be able to meet with you. You suggest that she ask at the tribal community center and at Abe's school if this could be set up for her. She learns that the Indian Health Service has a room in their clinic that can be used for this very purpose.

You begin meeting with Abe and Melissa. Abe is very guarded from the outset. They do not appear to trust you and are not forthcoming about what might have happened to change their academic results. It does not take long for you to become frustrated with the situation. You ask Melissa if the two of you can meet without Abe at your next meeting. She agrees to that. About midway through your session with her, you realize that you have failed to include an important source of information in your work with Abe. You ask Melissa if she thinks it would be useful for you to meet with Edward. She agrees that this might be useful. Your conversation with Edward goes like this:

Counselor: Edward, first off, I want to thank you for agreeing to meet with me. I also want to be sure you know that I'm concerned about Abe and hoping that you might be able to help shed some light on what has changed for them.

Edward: I share your concern about Abe. It was not until Melissa called me that I learned of their academic difficulties.

Counselor: It seems that everyone has been surprised by this change. I know that the two of you meet together once or twice a week.

Edward: Yes, we do. I really enjoy my time with Abe. They are very inquisitive and have a passion for learning.

Counselor: Can you say more about that?

Edward: Just the other day, we were taking a walk in the woods and I was pointing out different plants and the medicinal purpose they have. Abe was especially interested in the wide variety of plants and the ways in which they need to be prepared to have a medicinal effect.

Counselor: I know that it is typical in the Inuit culture for a child to be "born" into the work of an *angakkuq*, so in some ways, Abe is late coming to this work.

Edward: That is true, but sometimes in our tribe when we notice a special gift in a person, we have a history of working with that person. Abe is a good example of this. I have been paying close attention to their life and I see great potential for them.

Counselor: Can you say more about the journey for Abe? What needs to happen for them to become a shaman?

Edward: Well, Abe has only just started their apprenticeship. They will work with me for ten or more years to learn the customs and history of the tribe. They will also complete a personal journey sometimes called a quest. This time is used to help ensure that Abe is truly called to this work. I'll decide when this will happen along with the tribal leadership.

Counselor: Do you have an expectation about whether Abe should finish high school?

Edward: There is no expectation. Much of what Abe needs to know to do this work will be imparted in our work together. As I told Abe, I only completed the equivalent of sixth grade. So, no, there is no expectation. Things are different today than they were when I was a child. Given the way that Abe has come into this work, they would have more formal school than was expected of me.

Counselor: Is it possible that Abe has switched his academic focus from formal school to their work with you?

Edward: I suppose that is possible. Abe knows, though, that part of the reason we have begun meeting together is because of their academic success.

Counselor: To this point, I have struggled to have much of a conversation with Abe. They are a bit defensive and seem reluctant to open up to me. What suggestions do you have that might help me understand Abe's circumstances?

Edward: As a person who is not of the Inuit nation, you will typically be regarded as an outsider and people, like Abe, will be especially cautious. You must understand that we, the Inuit people, have been mistreated by many outsiders. This results in our being very cautious with others we are unfamiliar with.

Counselor: Of course, I can only imagine how difficult it is when someone arrives and supposedly has good intentions. How then might I frame the work I am doing to help Abe be a bit more trusting?

Edward: You might start by reintroducing yourself to Abe and providing him with some information about who you are and what is important for you. You'll be wise to stay away from how and where you were trained. Abe won't, at this point, be interested in that information. Talk to Abe, not at Abe, and share some personal information. That may help to break down the barriers you are facing.

Counselor: Thanks for this advice and for your time.

At the next session you meet again with Abe and their mother. Abe is still guarded, but you share information about your family and what brought you to your work in Alaska. It is not until you decide to meet alone with Abe that you begin to get a clearer picture of what has been happening for them. Abe shares that they are often teased and made fun of at school. They have not shared that with anyone because they do not see how doing so will help their situation. They admit that they have been skipping school. That is one reason why they are not performing well. They are not turning in homework nor are they participating in the in-class activities. Now that they realize they may be selected to be a shaman, they really only want to work with Edward. You talk about the importance of school and ask about the bullying. In time, Abe shares that they have been bullied by two other students for the past two years. Abe says the teachers never do anything about the mistreatment so "I just live with it." Abe says they are called names and forced to do things that are demeaning and sometimes painful (physically and emotionally).

Because Abe lives in such a small community, there is only one school for middle and high school. Abe would like to get away from these fellow students, but there really are not any options. They share with you that the teasing is about their academic ability, their gender identity, and now the bullies are also using his work with Edward as a way to hurt them. Abe begins crying and it is beginning to become clear why Abe is struggling academically.

Advocating for change

Over time, you begin to understand that Abe, though gifted, is not immune to the hateful treatment they have been experiencing. In working with Abe, you help them to develop their self-esteem in a manner that allows them to begin to stand up to the bullies or to report this behavior to their parents or the school administrators. At the same time, you begin to meet with school administrators and tribal leadership to create a policy that forbids bullying and provides appropriate punishment for such behavior at the school.

Although you live far from Abe you agree to journey to his town. You take advantage of being there and also meet with Edward, the school principal, and the tribal representative to the Inuit Circumpolar Council. In these meetings, you talk about the importance of having a zero-tolerance policy with regard to bullying (Gregory et al. 2010). This fits within the traditional laws of *maligait* (what has to be followed) and *tirigusuusiit* (what has to be avoided). The *angakkuq* might need to intervene if these traditional laws are broken.

EXPERT COMMENT

Although the therapist is eager to assist Abe in their journey, there were several considerations that resulted in some therapeutic success. First, the therapist learned to gain some cultural humility—or the notion they may not fully understand all of the cultural factors of the case or may not be trusted as someone outside of the community. Because of this, the therapist takes several preliminary steps to improve their relationship with Abe—including providing guidance in how to access teletherapy, speaking with Abe's mother separately, and even speaking with Edward (Abe's mentor and spiritual teacher). It was only through working with Edward that the therapist could gain some insight on how to be more effective in their work with Abe. If the therapist adamantly subscribed to, and maintained, Western definitions of boundaries, they would not have learned or benefited from the collective approaches that were crucial in this case.

Furthermore, one of the most commendable traits of the therapist is their ability to advocate for client. Too often, therapists (who use Western models of therapy) utilize individual talk therapy primarily as a way for clients to identify their core issues and learn ways to deal with their problems on their own. However, when dealing with issues related to systemic oppression, therapists could and should serve as social justice advocates and activists—particularly when working with youth and children who may not have the courage or voice to advocate for themselves. The counselor in this case should especially be commended for consulting tribal leadership for recommendations on laws and guidelines. In this way, the counselor is not just advocating for what they think is right, but rather what the client's community may collectively believe is right.

Taken together, the current case study is one that highlights the importance of centering intersectionality when working with clients. Although the client's gender identity may be a root cause for their bullying, it is evident that other multiple identities (e.g., race, ethnicity, spirituality, social class, geographic location, etc.) affect how their problems manifest or how therapy is conducted. For some historically marginalized groups, it is especially crucial to use intersectional approaches while maintaining cultural humility in order to ensure not only that the most effective treatment is being utilized, but also to avoid treatment that has been historically oppressive and harmful.

Expert comment authored by Kevin Nadal, PhD, New York, NY

Take-home messages

Bullying is far too common, and the consequences can be quite damaging for the target of bullying. One of the challenges faced by school administrators is, while there is an urgency to stop bullying, zero-tolerance measures have mixed results (Gregory et al. 2010). Nevertheless, bullying of LGBTQ+ people can be quite pervasive (Aragon et al. 2014; Espelage, Bosworth, and Simon 2000; Hatzenbuehler, Duncan, and Johnson 2015; Reisner et al. 2015).

Cultural humility and cultural competence are not the same thing. In this case example, we see how they both play out with the counselor. In the end, showing cultural humility is what allows the counselor to build a strong relationship with Abe. One aspect of our work as mental health providers is to advocate on behalf of our clients. In this case the advocacy happened at several levels, including tribal leadership.

CHAPTER 9

Trans Youth and Social Media

Social media has become a near-ubiquitous source of social interaction. More broadly, the internet has changed the ways in which people communicate with one another. As a result, many of the barriers that used to be in the way (e.g., distance, the need to make a long-distance phone call, the use of the postal service) of connecting with other people have been largely dismantled. As long as a person has a cellular phone and/or internet access, they can immediately connect with another person anywhere in the world using text, voice, or video technology.

For any marginalized community, the internet has allowed people to make connections that otherwise may not have been possible. Trans people have created web sites and other online resources designed to demystify the trans experience, provide referrals to competent and affirmative providers, and provide a social connection with others. All of these aspects of having an online presence have the potential to be beneficial for the user.

For trans youth, the internet can be a source of support, and it can also be a place where danger lurks. Unfortunately, some people are using the internet as a means for exploiting children and youth. A recent study reported that 67 percent of trans youth had participated in sex work (Wilson et al. 2009). This high incidence is likely informed by the risk of living with poverty, homelessness, discrimination, and violence. Many LGBTQ+ youth who end up living on the streets may feel as if their only option is to engage in "survival sex." Survival sex (also known as transactional sex) has been defined as engaging in sexual acts for the purpose of having a roof over your head or a meal to eat, rather than exchanging sex for money (Kattari and Begun 2017).

Exchanging money for sex is more common among people who engage in sex work. Survival sex does not necessarily include an exchange of money. LGBTQ+ youth are overrepresented in the number of youth that engage in sex work and also in the number of youth who are living on the streets or are homeless (Kattari and Begun 2017).

Details of the case

Natalia is a 14-year-old Latinx trans girl. She is living in a shelter for homeless youth in a large city not too far from her family home. Natalia has no contact with her father and very limited contact with her mother. Natalia has been living as a trans girl since she left her family home. Her father made it very clear that she was not welcome in the home. The youth shelter has ten beds, and the youth are eligible to stay in the shelter for 60 days with the possibility of a 30-day extension. The extension is based on the need for a place to live and documented progress of life activities including attending school. Natalia has been in the youth shelter for seven days. She has a good knowledge of the rules of the shelter and of what she is expected to do. The shelter residents are allowed to have a cell phone and Natalia's mother covers the expenses of Natalia's phone.

One of the reasons why Natalia left her family home was the edict her father gave her. He fell just short of physically assaulting her and Natalia remains traumatized by their last interaction. In addition to the physical threat, he also yelled at Natalia using harsh, cutting language.

Exploring clinical material

You work for a community mental health center that provides counseling services to residents of multiple homeless shelters in the area. Company policy requires that you conduct an intake with new residents of the shelter within seven days of admission. Today is Natalia's seventh day and she is scheduled to meet with you after school. School is held either in the shelter or at a nearby school depending on the academic needs of the student. If a student has an Individualized Education Plan (IEP), they attend the local school. Otherwise, they receive their educational training in the shelter. The shelter serves adolescents between the ages of 12 and 18.

During the intake session with Natalia you ask her about her trauma history. You notice Natalia becomes even more withdrawn than usual. You are aware Natalia frequently ran away from home prior to being placed in the shelter. Eventually she would return with the support of her mother. As a part of the intake paperwork, you know Natalia has social media profiles on the following apps: TikTok, Instagram, and Snapchat. As a condition of staying in the shelter, the youth are required to give access to their accounts to a member of the shelter staff. You have reason to believe Natalia was not completely honest with the staff and that she has one or more additional login IDs for social media and dating apps. This violates shelter rules both because Natalia was not forthcoming about these IDs but also because they are dating apps (a different type of social media per the shelter rules).

You realize, in your third meeting with Natalia, that she has had an increasing number of unaccounted-for absences from the shelter. Natalia attends a local middle school as she has a history of ADHD. There are four residents who attend this school. They have been told to meet at the front entrance to the school and to leave for the shelter no more than ten minutes after the closing school bell. If one or more of the students have been disciplined during the day, that information is communicated directly with shelter staff. Natalia, for the past three days, has arrived back at the shelter 30 or more minutes after her peers.

Even though Natalia tends to be tight-lipped about her whereabouts and the traumatic experiences she encountered prior to coming to the shelter, you have worked to develop a caring relationship built on trust. One aspect of this trust is related to your consistency in Natalia's life. You do not make promises you cannot keep, and you make sure to check in on her in a way that is supportive rather than punitive. Consider the following conversation, which happened on Natalia's 15th day in the shelter.

Counselor: Hi Natalia.

Natalia: Hello.

Counselor: How was school today?

Natalia: Fine.

Counselor: I know you had a midterm exam today. How do you think that went?

Natalia: Not very well. I really don't like history. It feels like all we ever do is memorize dates and names. None of it seems to relate to me.

Counselor: I remember how hard history classes were for me. I can relate to what you are saying.

Natalia: Yeah, but you're so much smarter than I am.

Counselor: I am not sure I agree with you. You probably already know this, but I was a high school dropout. Between the abuse I experienced in foster homes and the challenges I was having in school, I couldn't stay in school.

Natalia: I knew you had dropped out and lived here a while ago, but still–you've been to graduate school–I'm not sure I'll even be able to finish high school, let alone go to college.

Counselor: Would you like to go to college Natalia?

Natalia: Maybe. When I was younger, I wanted to be a nurse.

Counselor: A nurse? What do you like about that?

Natalia: [Natalia shrugs her shoulders.] I think I liked the idea that nurses help other people. You know, when I go to a doctor's office the nurse checks my heart and lungs and stuff like that. The part I don't think I'd like is giving someone a shot. I don't think I'd want to do something I know would hurt another person.

Counselor: That makes sense. I think I feel the same way.

After this opening conversation, you begin to talk with Natalia about her activities after school and the reasons why she arrives at the shelter later than her peers. Natalia again becomes withdrawn. You gently question Natalia and remind her it would be better if she told the truth than for you to find out she has been dishonest. Eventually Natalia confides in you that before she came to the shelter, she would frequently be on the street overnight. On those evenings she often stayed with a man named Gordon. Natalia would not tell you anything else about Gordon except that she stays in touch with him using WhatsApp. She admits she refers to him as Uncle Gordon at his request. She also says one of things he helps her with is access to hormones. She likes being on hormones and knows she would never be able to get consent from her parents to start them. When asked about the nature of her interactions with Gordon, Natalia says, "He is so sweet to me. He brings me flowers and other presents. This is in addition to the hormones." You ask Natalia what it is that Gordon expects in return. You are aware your session has run longer than normal, but you also realize that Natalia is finally opening up to you. Natalia answers sometimes she has sex with Gordon but not every time.

General commentary

At this point in your work with Natalia you are concerned for her safety and her interactions with "Uncle Gordon." You let her know she will not have cell phone privileges until you are able to get to the bottom of what is happening in her life. You are unable to report what is happening to Natalia to Child Protective Services because you do not know who Gordon is. You are not even sure that is his first name. Still, you are very aware it is likely Natalia is being sexually exploited.

- Depending on how Natalia arrived at the shelter (e.g., runaway, parental rights severed), there may be a need to reach out to her parents. Natalia appears to have an established "relationship" with an adult in which she is being sexually exploited. Since this relationship predates Natalia's connection with the shelter, it may be important to notify her parents.

An affirmative approach to counseling

Youth who end up on the streets open themselves up to being taken advantage of (Halcón and Lifson 2004). This is what happened with Natalia. She met Gordon through another friend and Gordon quickly set the expectations for how and when they would interact. Gordon had a good understanding of what would keep Natalia engaged with him. He knew, for instance, that Natalia had always wanted to be on hormones. By offering to supply her with hormones, Gordon knew that Natalia would feel obligated to engage in sexual acts. It will be important to determine the source of the hormones. More important is the need to engage in a harm reduction (Dietz and Halem 2016; Ehrbar and Gorton 2010; Winters and Ehrbar 2010) approach to Natalia's situation. For trans people, a harm-reduction approach involves ensuring that the trans person is receiving a safe supply of hormones and they are engaging in the necessary medical treatment to ensure the hormone levels are in a therapeutic range. Checking a person's labs is a critical part of medical treatment for trans people. This starts with baseline values and additional labs are drawn at 3, 6, 9, and 12 months in the first year of treatment (Deutsch and Buchholz 2015). After that, labs can be drawn annually or as needed.

Natalia may need trauma-based or trauma-informed treatment. Use of a tool such as an analysis of Adverse Childhood Experiences (ACES) (Felitti et al. 1998) will allow you to begin to create a picture of the way trauma has impacted Natalia. Natalia may need time to feel safe exploring the trauma she has experienced. If there is any way to determine who "Uncle Gordon" is and make a report on him that would also be important.

EXPERT COMMENT

As I write my response to this chapter, most of us are currently required to "Shelter in Place" as we collectively battle this tragic public health crisis that is the COVID-19 pandemic. Perhaps, for the first time, we cisgender individuals finally know what it feels like to be socially and physically isolated from our peers and loved ones.

Physical and emotional safety is always a priority for children. As a therapist who has worked in group homes with transition-aged youth, I understand well how balancing the program's community cohesion with individual treatment needs for youth who suffer from complex trauma is a formidable challenge. In Natalia's case, the explanation behind her long history of running away is unclear, but we might assume that she had to leave, and doing so put her at great risk for harm. From this perspective, kicking her out of the shelter likely would be a re-enactment, a recapitulation of trauma (e.g., "If you do not do as we say, you will need to leave and go back to the streets where danger awaits you").

I wish caring for Natalia were as simple as taking her phone away. In doing so, however, we likely do more damage than good. Punishments and loss of privileges typically lead to power struggles—losing battles for parents or institutions insisting on compliance. I agree with the need to prioritize Natalia's needs according to risk. In this way, we can integrate a gender-affirming, harm-reduction approach while implementing trauma-informed interventions that take minority stress theory into consideration.

Being honest with ourselves: young people can and will access all kinds of technology regardless of limits placed on them by authority figures. They do not need a phone to find themselves in harm's way. Yes, taking the phone away would create a temporary barrier between Natalia and those who aim to exploit her. Yet by taking her phone away, we also naïvely avoid reality and make her vulnerable to greater risk on the street. People like "Uncle Gordon," who prey especially on trans and queer youth, are always a few steps ahead of us. Uncle Gordon will not simply go away because Natalia's phone is gone. He will buy her a new one and have even more leverage to isolate her from those who are in a position to help. Taking the phone represents a lost opportunity to provide connection and critical interventions that will prevent her from experiencing further harm.

What can we do? First, we need to prioritize Natalia's needs. Natalia ought to remain in the shelter in order to ensure she has secure, safe housing. There, she can continue to build a working relationship with her providers who have her best interests in mind. The relationship they develop will offer a safe haven within which she can build her self-esteem, progress along her gender journey, and build resiliency.

Natalia needs access to medical care including safer sex education. Trans youth generally will find the means to get their hormones. We need to help them access a safe and informed path and with guidance and monitoring by a medical gender specialist. Using a trauma-informed approach to treatment will be useful for building a trusting alliance with Natalia and, focusing on her basic stability, she will develop the psychological resources to engage in the reflective work that will lead to a change in her behavior. At this early stage, family treatment is not recommended as it could expose Natalia to further abuse by her father and might compromise her safety.

It seems likely that Natalia continues to leave home to protect herself from shame, guilt, and abuse. Notably, she also demonstrates hope and optimism for a new life. She is confronted with becoming her authentic gendered self, but at a cost. Given her circumstances, she is in a survival state of mind and vulnerable to the influence of others—Uncle Gordon, her perpetrator, provides the resources, attention, and security she craves with the aim of grooming her. He has become Natalia's new "caretaker." Sexually exploited youth are often manipulated by their perpetrators, who reassure victims that they are special and provide them with a false sense of nurturance (Halcón and Lifson 2004). Rather than asserting a hard boundary that will lead Natalia back to the streets, we should strive to stay connected and build trust with her. In this way, we can engage collaboratively in the development of an "action plan" that will lean toward wellness while she builds up her sense of self-worth and resiliency. Through means of empowerment, she will be able to make decisions that are aligned with her safety and holistic well-being. The aim is to help Natalia develop the kind of internal stability and security to make it possible for her to respond skillfully versus reacting impulsively to the decisions that confront her. From this point of view, we're creating options for connection: Uncle Gordon hopefully will not be the only resource available when Natalia is struggling. She also can reach out to her therapist.

Expert comment authored by Karisa Barrow, PsyD, Oakland, CA

Take-home messages

Adolescents may be at risk in ways other trans people are not. Adolescents may have access to a cell phone. If this is the case, it is important to set clear expectations about how the phone can be used. This includes having a responsible adult check the adolescent's usage history. It is not really important to know how many hours the phone is used, rather the kinds and types of apps that are on the phone. Even though apps like Facebook seem relatively harmless, it is very easy for a person to troll the application looking for vulnerable people who they can take advantage of. Like in the case of Natalia, it is easy for someone to befriend a trans adolescent and take advantage of them over time. Initially the relationship may seem harmless. However, it is always important to ask why an adult is befriending an adolescent to whom they have no logical connection (e.g., family member).

One of the challenges in setting limitations on an adolescent's use of social media is that often the adolescent may know more about the technology than the adult who is overseeing their use. As a result, the adult may or may not know where to look to determine if the adolescent is engaging in potentially dangerous behavior. There are some cues and tools that may help the adult to determine if there might be problematic behavior. First, is the adolescent making it difficult to access their phone? This may be a signal there is something there they do not want you to see. Second, you can easily set up phone finder applications that can find the adolescent's phone and track a person's whereabouts. Some might say this is too much oversight and that adolescents need to be given the space to learn how to behave without putting themselves at risk. Obviously, if the adolescent has turned off their phone these features will no longer be available. It may be important to create a log of the times when the phone is off. If there is a pattern to this, it may be time to have a conversation about what is happening during those times.

In addition to understanding the types of access trans adolescents have to technology, it is important to gain a clear understanding of the kinds of abuse a trans person has experienced. Trauma-informed treatment is one aspect of affirmative care for trans people (Richmond, Burnes, and Carroll 2012). It may take some time to develop the kind of relationship that allows for the trans client to feel safe enough to discuss their trauma history. Exploring trauma from childhood into the presenting age of the client will allow providers to gain an understanding of how trauma has impacted a trans client's life. In addition to the types of trauma experienced by cisgender people (e.g., sexual abuse, neglect, physical abuse), trans people may also find that typical developmental processes, including puberty, are traumatic. Puberty represents a time in a person's life when their body changes in a number of ways that feel inconsistent with a person's felt gender identity. Trans people may at best be curious about the changes in their body and at worst be repulsed by what is happening. When a trans client's reaction falls toward repulsion, there can be far-reaching implications moving forward in life. Added to this may be mistreatment within a client's family of origin. Unfortunately, trans feminine children are often at risk of physical and sexual abuse. This can come from a parent or guardian, a sibling, another family member, or a trusted community leader (e.g., clergy or a youth group leader). This case is focused on an adolescent who is being sexually exploited, but providers must also attend to abuse that a person might have experienced in early childhood.

• CHAPTER 10 •

Sexuality Exploration

Many things happen during adolescence. This can be a time when a young person begins to explore their sexuality (Hock 2012). Youth are often willing to explore options for their sexuality that adults in their life are not familiar with. For example, in the 1960s through the end of the century there were three options that a person might have taken in declaring their sexual identity: gay, straight, or bisexual. Everyone would assume that a person was heterosexual unless they declared otherwise, and coming out as a sexual minority has not always been a simple process.

Sexual orientation options today are much broader than they were when Harry Benjamin (1966) first classified trans people. Among the options people identify with now are heterosexual (straight), gay, lesbian, bisexual, pansexual, and asexual. There can be variations of each of these identities, including having a fluid sexual orientation (Diamond 2008). Additionally, it is important to remember that a person's sexual behavior may be different than their sexual orientation. For example, a person may engage in same sex/gender behaviors but identify as straight.

Details of the case

Evelyn is a 19-year-old Korean American. She was assigned male at birth and her parents gave her the name Watson. Evelyn refers to this as her dead name.[4] Evelyn graduated from high school last spring. She has been out as a trans identified person since middle school. She has been on hormones for about 12 months and is scheduled for an orchiectomy in six months.

Evelyn identifies as pansexual. She states that she is currently in a polyamorous relationship with a cisgender, queer woman (Amelia) and a trans man (Logan) who has a pansexual identity. Evelyn states that she was first in a relationship with Amelia and that they recently invited Logan to join their family. Even though their family group is relatively new, they have agreed on loving, healthy boundaries for their relationship. At this time, they have agreed to keep their relationship between the three of them, meaning that no one will step outside of the relationship and they will not include others.

Exploring clinical material

Evelyn has been seeing you for counseling for about six months. You are the only provider in the area who has any experience with trans clients, and you feel ill equipped to understand Evelyn's sexual identity. While you were in graduate school, you had planned to become a certified sex therapist through the American Association of Sexuality Educators, Counselors, and Therapists (AASECT). As you got closer to completing the training process, you realized you did not need this certification to work with trans people. As a result, you did not renew your membership with AASECT.

It has only been recently that Evelyn has begun talking about having a pansexual identity and that she is now in a polyamorous relationship. As Evelyn first talked about these identities, you felt lost, as you had never heard the terms pansexual or polyamorous. You assumed polyamorous meant Evelyn wanted to be married to more than one person.

Evelyn: Hello.

Counselor: Hi, how have you been?

Evelyn: I'm doing pretty good. I really like the way things are going in my relationship. I moved in with Amelia and Logan will be moving in next month.

Counselor: Tell me more about how things are working in your relationship. I have to admit, this isn't an area of expertise for me. After our last session, I had to look up some of the terms you used—pansexual and polyamorous. Would it be okay if I asked you what those terms mean to you?

Evelyn: Thanks for asking—you looked a little bit lost last week. For me, pansexual means that I am attracted to people because of who they are, and their gender does not matter to me. I might be in a relationship with a person who is trans, cisgender, is or isn't on the gender binary—I am attracted to the person because maybe we have consistent values and beliefs. Does that make sense?

Counselor: It does. I guess I've never really given much thought to why people are attracted to one another. I think maybe, for me anyway, as a cisgender, heterosexual person, I've never really had to spend much time thinking about how gender plays a role in romantic relationships.

Evelyn: Right. Most people never have to think about this. It'll be nice when we are all living together.

Counselor: That is the polyamory part, right? Being in a relationship with more than one person?

Evelyn: Yes. I have to say this is all pretty new for me too. I first met Amelia last year. She graduated a year ahead of me, but we stayed in touch. We didn't really start dating until after I turned 18.

Counselor: You have talked about her before, but I guess I didn't realize things had become quite so serious.

Evelyn: Our first official date was on Valentine's Day. She told me we were going to go out to dinner. We had a sweet time and she even invited me to come over to her apartment overnight. I wasn't sure my parents would go for that. They are giving me more leeway now that I am over 18, but I didn't want to push that too far.

Counselor: Have your parents met Amelia?

Evelyn: They met her on Valentine's Day since she picked me up at my parent's house.

Counselor: Tell me more about Logan and how he became involved with you and Amelia...

General commentary

Exploring sexuality is an important developmental process. Adolescents are often left to their own devices when it comes to learning about sex, sexuality, and sexual behaviors. The type of sex education in schools varies from one state to the next. For some adolescents, all they learn about is abstinence (Nelson 2016). In those same states, there are high rates of unplanned pregnancies among teenagers. The challenge for adolescents is to find accurate sources of information, which may not be their parents. Too often, teens rely on one another for information and this information may or may not be accurate. Sex education is a politically charged topic. Many people believe education should happen within the family and not in schools. Adolescents may be at risk of getting inaccurate information even if it is coming from their parents.

Sex and gender are separate but interrelated concepts (American Psychological Association 2015). Simply put, sex is about biology, and gender is about a person's identity. Sex, then, is about chromosomes, genitalia, and hormones. Gender is about the way a person wears their hair, the clothing they wear, and the myriad rules about how to behave based on their perceived sex. Mistakes are often made by people regarding another person's sex. For example, a person who was assigned female at birth may be mistaken for a man in the women's restroom. This may seem like a harmless mistake, but this type of interaction could quickly escalate into an act of violence directed at the person who is assumed to be in the wrong restroom.

Everyone has a sexual orientation or identity. Sexual orientation today is much broader than it was 30, 40, or 50 years ago. The majority of people are heterosexual (straight). A much smaller group of people identify as gay, lesbian, or queer.[5] These terms are generally thought to originate from white culture. This means that LGBTQ+ people of color (POC) may not use these terms. Added to this is the reality that LGBTQ+ POC may also feel pressure from cultural expectations. This may include religious beliefs, family obligations, and rites of passage.

Everyone also has a gender identity. For some people, gender identity is a very personal way to designate how they see themselves as a gendered person. Most people spend little time considering what gender means to them. People whose gender identity is consistent with the sex they were assigned at birth are known as cisgender people.

Cisgender people rarely have to think about what their gender is in the same way that heterosexual people rarely contemplate their sexual orientation.

An affirmative approach to counseling

Using a sex-positive approach to counseling is the best way to address this client's needs. One of the major challenges to using a sex-positive approach to counseling is that few training programs offer courses in human sexuality, and those that do may not require the participants to take the course in order to complete the program (Burnes, Singh, and Witherspoon 2017). Burnes et al. (2017) define sex positivity as "individuals and communities who emphasize openness, nonjudgmental attitudes, freedom, and liberation about sexuality and sexual expression" (p.471). It is possible that some training programs cover sexual dysfunction as a part of a psychopathology course (or another course that addresses diagnosis and the *DSM-5*) (Burnes et al. 2017). If a trainee receives training only in sexual dysfunction, they are unlikely to use a sex-positive approach to counseling.

In using a sex-positive approach, providers must include cultural humility in the ways they interact with their clients (Burnes 2017; Burnes and Stanley 2017). The use of cultural humility involves the need to interrogate one's own beliefs and knowledge related to individual differences (e.g., race/ethnicity, socioeconomic status, disability, sexual orientation, gender identity). A sex-positive approach also maintains that sex is healthy as long as it is "safe, consensual, and communicative" (Burnes 2017, p.175). Burnes goes on to say that creative explorations of sexual behavior are healthy and that providers should not pathologize clients who are exploring their sexuality and the kinds of sex practices they find to be enjoyable.

Sex positivity also approaches work with clients by understanding they may not have received a solid foundation of knowledge about sex, sexuality, and sexual behaviors. As a result, it is important to be open and gentle with clients as they begin to explore their sexuality. It is just as important to identify sex-negative attitudes and influences. For some clients, especially trans and non-binary people, the lessons learned in their family of origin may have significant negative impacts on how they think about themselves as a sexual being.

EXPERT COMMENT

One of the most important guiding principles in working with clients around sexual and gender health is not to make assumptions. This becomes especially relevant for mental health professionals who, in all likelihood, have had little to no advanced training in human sexuality, yet a lifetime of exposure to sexual misinformation and cultural biases. For example, being pansexual (a sexual orientation that denotes romantic and/or physical attractions) is not the same as being polyamorous (a type of relationship structure, also referred to as consensual non-monogamy or CNM). It is critical that mental health providers avoid the trap of conflating these related, but distinct, aspects of identity and behavior. Evelyn's counselor was appropriate in asking for clarification about these terms. These are topics, however, that often require specialized knowledge and training. If lacking, we are ethically bound to educate ourselves further, seek out supervision or consultation, and/or consider referral to a more competent provider (American Psychological Association 2017).

An assumption that is not fully addressed in Evelyn's case is whether she has become sexually active with any of her partners. Just because Evelyn is in relationships with Amelia and Logan does not necessarily mean that she is sexual with either person. As a counselor, it is important to get comfortable asking clients about sexual health-related questions (e.g., "Have either of your relationships become sexual? [If yes] How so?"). In this way, we can avoid making assumptions about sexual health, including assumptions about frequency and type of activity. Such questions also pave the way for further discussion related to gender affirmation (or dysphoria) via physical contact with others.

Mental health providers can play a very important role in helping clients identify healthy and appropriate relational boundaries, whether this involves monogamy or polyamory. In Evelyn's case, it would be helpful to clarify what exactly she means in saying that "no one will step outside" of her relationships. Does this involve a restriction on sexual contact outside the three partners? What about dating others without sexual contact? Flirting? Fantasizing about others while engaged in self-stimulation? The spectrum of "stepping out"—that is, relational boundaries—can be wide. Rather than assume meaning, it is important to clarify with clients in order to best understand their relationship experiences and expectations.

Finally, it is critical to discuss with clients the sexual health implications of transition-related medical interventions (e.g., hormone therapy, surgeries). Ideally, in Evelyn's case, she has had such conversations with her medical providers. Research shows, however, that this is unfortunately uncommon (Coleman et al. 2011). For example, hormone therapy (depending on dose and duration) often results in changes to libido, changes in physical sensations, reduced ability to achieve and/or maintain erections, and changes in the amount and consistency of ejaculate. These changes may be distressing if clients are unprepared for them. Alternatively, many such sexual changes are welcome and may help to reduce gender dysphoria. Again, it is important not to make assumptions; rather, ask your client what sexual changes they may have experienced and what reaction(s) this has raised for them.

Expert comment authored by Jennifer A. Vencill, PhD, Rochester, MN

Take-home messages

This case presents one of the many ways in which a person might explore and express their sexuality. Evelyn is in a polyamorous (CNM) relationship. Even though this is a new experience for her, there is no reason for the provider to do anything but support Evelyn.

We see how the provider owns their lack of knowledge. This is not the first time we have seen this from a provider. The provider acknowledges their lack of knowledge and addresses the ways they have worked to close their knowledge gap. Equally important is that the provider checked with the client to ensure that what they learned matched the client's lived experience.

PART THREE

Adulthood

CHAPTER 11

Workplace Issues

Most adults spend about one-third of their day at work. Typically, people have completed training for these jobs in the hopes that it will be a lifelong career, regardless of whether it is with the same employer. Trans people gained protection against discrimination in the United States in 2020 when the U.S. Supreme Court ruled that existing laws protect LGBTQ people from employment discrimination. This does not mean a trans person won't experience violence, sexual harassment, or other types of mistreatment. In this chapter I explore challenges that might be faced by trans people in the workplace.

Details of the case

Joon-Woo is a first-generation Korean American. He was assigned female at birth and is 37 years old. Joon-Woo completed a bachelor's degree in accounting and passed all parts of the Certified Public Accountant (CPA) exam on the first try. Joon-Woo works for a large accounting firm and has been on track for a management-level position.

Exploring clinical material

Joon-Woo (formerly Ji-Woo) began work at a large accounting firm as an intern during college. Joon-Woo was offered a job after graduation and has worked in several divisions of the firm, including auditing, tax, and consulting. Joon-Woo has been in the consulting division for the past ten years and enjoys the work. One of the reasons why this work has been so meaningful is because Joon-Woo is able to work on the contracts with Korean customers.

Prior to making a medical transition (hormones and top surgery), Joon-Woo was a mid-level manager in the global advisory services department. In this position, Joon-Woo traveled quarterly to South Korea. In part because of his medical transition (surgery), Joon-Woo has not made a trip to South Korea for the past six months. During the most recent employee evaluation, Joon-Woo received a poor evaluation. His manager was unable to provide specific examples as to why Joon-Woo's work was unacceptable. Joon-Woo sought advice from a colleague in another division. This colleague acknowledged Joon-Woo's concerns and said they had begun hearing rumors about Joon-Woo and the ways their manager viewed trans people. Joon-Woo did not take much time to consider whether his accounting firm would be supportive. It turns out they are one of the few firms that does not have protection in place for employment discrimination.

Joon-Woo has gone from being a very skilled, self-assured employee to one who doubts his abilities and is constantly looking over his shoulder to make sure he is not being watched by his supervisor. This sense of paranoia has escalated for Joon-Woo and he has begun taking at least one day off work each week. Now, in addition to the poor work evaluation, his supervisor has placed him on probation for high absenteeism.

Joon-Woo seeks out support through his Employee Assistance Program (EAP). He is assigned to your caseload. You have little training on how to work with trans people but are the recognized expert on career issues in your local office. When Joon-Woo comes in to see you, he states that the reason for seeking care was due to difficult experiences at work. On further exploration, you determine that Joon-Woo's concerns stem from changes in management attitudes since Joon-Woo's transition. Joon-Woo reports that he loves the work he was doing at the firm and does not want to lose this job. He has worked for this firm for over 15 years. In your work with Joon-Woo, you normalize his experiences and help him to think of other types of work he might conduct in another division of his firm. Because you only have three sessions with Joon-Woo according to the EAP plan, you provide him with his options for continuing care with you or being referred to another provider in the community.

Workplace discrimination

Discrimination in the workplace can be a common yet difficult-to-prove situation for trans people. Further, when one works for an employer who does not provide nondiscrimination protection, there may be a feeling that it does not matter what you can or cannot prove. Being supportive of your client's experience is critical. As we see in Joon-Woo's case, he has become impaired by the climate set by his supervisor. Joon-Woo is no longer confident of his abilities in this workplace.

The challenge for Joon-Woo, and for other transgender people, is whether or not a lateral move to another division will be favorable. Joon-Woo has the skills to work in other areas, but he may not feel any different given the conservative climate. If Joon-Woo also lives in a conservative part of the country, he may need to consider relocating to another office with the firm. Even though this will not change the company policy, it is possible that Joon-Woo will feel more accepted by his supervisor and co-workers.

There have been changes in the landscape of employment discrimination in recent years. Led in part by Vandy Beth Glenn, who sued her employer (the State of Georgia) for wrongful termination, there has been a change in how gender is applied to discrimination cases (Lambda Legal n.d.). Specifically, under Title IX the courts have deemed that discrimination based on gender is against the law and applies to trans people (NCTE 2020a). This decision came during the Obama administration. Recently the U.S. Supreme Court handed down a favorable decision regarding employment discrimination against trans people. The decision cited the 1964 Civil Rights Act (Library of Congress 2016) and stated that sex is a protected class that is inclusive of LGBTQ+ people.

Other workplace concerns

Discrimination in the workplace is just one issue trans people are often faced with. I explore other challenges that happen in the workplace in the following areas. Readers are encouraged to explore information available from Lambda Legal and from the National Center for Transgender Equality for up-to-date policies and resources on this topic.

Locker rooms, restrooms, and uniforms. One area of concern is related to the ways that facilities are divided based on a person's actual or perceived gender. Most places of employment offer restrooms or have locker rooms that are sex segregated. That is to say, there is one space designated for men or males and another for women or females. The obvious issue here is that a person with a non-binary identity or a person who is in the midst of a transition–be it medical, social, or legal–may not be able to easily locate a space in which they feel safe or welcomed. It may be difficult to address this if the employer does not have any policies that protect trans employees. Ideally, the trans person will be allowed to use the restroom or locker room that fits with their own sense of gender. Alternatively, if there is space that is not gendered (i.e., identified as being for male or female people), the trans person may feel more comfortable in this space.

Uniforms at work may bring another source of distress. If the organization has different uniforms for women than they do for men, this may be an issue for a trans person, especially someone with a non-binary identity. There may not be an easy solution to this issue. Although in this situation there is no need to build a new space as there might be with restrooms, a trans employee may feel very uncomfortable working in clothing that is inconsistent with their identity.

Name changes and other records. Name changes may or may not be a simple process depending on where a person lives and works. It is possible that an employer will not allow an official (or unofficial) name change without legal evidence of the change. However, if cisgender people are allowed to use nicknames, there is no reason why a trans person should not be allowed to as well. Although the nickname a trans person uses may not be another form of their given name (e.g., Rob for Robert or Mickie for Michelle), trans people should not be treated any differently than their cisgender colleagues.

Health insurance. There are two general concerns regarding health insurance. The first is whether the employee wants their gender marker changed with their insurance company. Second is whether there is insurance coverage for trans health needs.

A trans person may choose not to change their gender marker through human resources as they want to be able to access healthcare that is associated with gendered procedures. For example, a person who was assigned male cannot get a hysterectomy. The insurance company would likely deny a claim for coverage as the healthcare industry assumes that certain care is based on a person's gender. This can be tricky for the trans person, and they will likely receive a more favorable response if they work for an employer that has affirming policies. Some insurance companies recognize that a provider is treating the organ systems that are present, meaning that a trans male would have a referral for a hysterectomy approved given medical necessity.

The second issue, whether or not the health plan covers transition-related healthcare, can be complicated. When a person is considering accepting a job with a new employer, they may not want to "out" themselves in the onboarding process. However, it may be difficult, if not impossible, to find out the details of insurance coverage without doing so. In some cases, an insurance plan may both exclude coverage for trans-related care and state that such care is not medically necessary. Insurance companies do not pay for services that are not medically necessary. Most professional health organizations have deemed transition-related care to be medically necessary. It is also important for your client to know that just because an employer has a health plan from a specific insurer (e.g., Aetna, Blue Cross Blue Shield) does not mean the policy will have the necessary coverage. Each business negotiates the types of coverage that their health policy will include. It is this negotiation that sets the price for premiums. Employee A, who works for Company Z, may have coverage through a specific insurer and trans care is offered. Employee B, who works for Company Y may have the same insurer, but the plan may exclude care. A recent executive order in the United States gutted the protections against mistreatment in medical settings. The rule that was in place, Section 1557, was a part of the Affordable Care Act.

References and reference checking. Employers typically ask for three or more references prior to making a job offer. A trans person may have three people who can provide a solid reference, but if these people do not know about the trans person's name or pronouns, the conversation with the prospective employer may not go very well. As an example, I was once asked to provide a reference for a former student. This student used the non-binary pronouns of they/them/their. As I was talking with the prospective employer, I used these pronouns since that is what I knew. The person completing the reference check was confused by this. I was able to play off my use of "they" without outing my former student. However, if you are working with someone who is seeking employment, it may be useful to have a discussion about how and when to use references and the importance of preparing the reference provider to ensure they have a current understanding of their transition status.

Assessing workplace climate. The American Psychological Association for Graduate Students (APAGS) has developed a climate guide to assist people in making decisions about whether an employer or other entity has LGBTQ+ affirming policies and practices (APAGS Committee on Sexual Orientation and Gender Diversity 2018). This simple guide provides a list of questions across seven domains. The domains are (a) external environment, (b) organizational track record, (c) leadership, (d) mission and strategy, (e) organizational culture, (f) structure, and (g) systems (policies and procedures). After answering the questions, the user can then "grade" the organization. Although this is a very subjective tool, users may find it helpful as they may be asking themselves questions they had not given consideration to through the job application and interview process.

Retraining. Some trans people will find that the work they were engaged in prior to transition no longer fits their career needs. For example, some trans women make a "flight to masculinity" prior to coming out as a female. This flight to masculinity means they are working in a career field typically completed by men (e.g., law enforcement, firefighting, construction trades, military). They may decide they would like to get training in a new career field because their interests have changed or because they do not think they will be safe continuing in the previous line of work (e.g., they fear for their safety from co-worker sabotage). Retraining can be expensive and time consuming. Completing the process may be worth the effort as it will ensure that the individual is happy in the work they are conducting.

EXPERT COMMENT

In reading the case, what resonated most was Joon-Woo's passion for the opportunities granted to him by his current position, namely, the opportunity to work with Korean clients and colleagues. The next important component involved the timing of his job evaluation, which consequently negatively affected his attendance at work. The timing of his attendance problems coincided directly with learning of his supervisor's negative attitudes toward transgender people. My recommendations are centered on these two segments of the case.

Cultural alignment in working with Korean clients

As a Korean American, Joon-Woo had the opportunity to attune his work in an international context that was aligned with his personal experience. The details of this work are not known but I would suspect that Joon-Woo was able to speak Korean, stay up to date about Korean culture and the specific ways the country's laws and/or policies impacted his direct work, as well as to have the opportunity to connect with individuals of his ethnic background thereby sharing cultural values and/or traditions that were likely not available to him in other aspects of his job. The loss of this opportunity is significant and should not be overlooked. It is also important to consider whether his supervisor is of Korean descent (plausible given the linguistic and cultural demands of the job). To face rejection related to his transgender identity from a Korean supervisor and potential elder may be especially difficult for Joon-Woo. His career counselor should inquire about the cultural dynamics of the supervisory relationship and larger firm, and whether Joon-Woo feels a conflict of allegiance (feeling he must conceal his transgender identity to maintain his racial, ethnic community) in having to choose a new firm or position that removes him from his Korean colleagues and clients.

Timing of negative job evaluation

Joon-Woo's attendance at work began to suffer after he learned that his supervisor was not supportive of his transition, especially given the supervisor's inability to provide evidence for his negative evaluation. The actual functions of the job, colleagues, and larger firm appear to remain positive for Joon-Woo. In fact, he is able to confide in a colleague about his experiences and to access the EAP to cope with the situation. A major challenge here is whether Joon-Woo's evaluation and attendance are known by the entire firm. It is unknown whether he would receive similar treatment in another department or whether he has support from higher administration to intervene on his behalf in his current position. At the same time, Joon-Woo has years of positive evaluations and job skills that would help him on the job market should he choose to leave his firm. He could consult with a headhunter to identify firms that are known to have positive work environments for LGBTQ+ people and have the opportunity to work with Korean clients. I would also encourage him to seek out online networks of LGBTQ+ CPAs that can help him navigate his current conditions and/or build his network should he choose to pursue another firm.

Expert comment authored by Alison Cerezo, PhD, Santa Barbara, CA

Take-home messages

Given that people spend one-third or more of their day in their jobs, it is important to find work that is meaningful and safe. Reminding your clients that there can be great variability in the climate of a workplace will help them to manage their expectations about the job. Ideally, everyone would be able to find work that is meaningful and safe, but those two aspects do not always work hand in hand.

Helping our clients to explore career options can be an important task. If you have never received career counseling training, it will be important to have a referral source who is able to provide this. Career assessment is a specialized type of assessment that is primarily mastered by psychologists in the field of counseling psychology.

The focus of this chapter—workplace issues—is a reminder that the landscape for protection of trans people can (and does) change very quickly. On Friday, June 12, 2020, the Trump administration gutted Section 1557 of the Patient Protection and Affordable Care Act (U.S. Department of Health and Human Services 2020). First established in 2010, Section 1557 was the nondiscrimination section of the Affordable Care Act. Although this rule was suspended regarding sexual orientation and gender identity, the final ruling (and its timing) were a difficult blow to the LGBTQ+ community. Only three days later, on Monday, June 15, 2020 the U.S. Supreme Court decision about discrimination employment directed at LGBTQ+ people was against the law. All this to say: laws, rules, regulation, and guidelines can change very quickly. It is for this reason that it is vitally important to keep up to date on these issues.

CHAPTER 12

Becoming a Trans Parent

M any people have a strong desire to become a parent. They may find this role to be fulfilling as they have the chance to help shape the life of another person. There are some important considerations that a trans person may want to keep in mind if parenting is an important life task. In this chapter I explore the ways in which a person can become a parent and how that may be challenging for a trans person. I also explore how a medical transition may impact the ability to become a parent using one's own genetic material.

Details of the case

Jalen is a 24-year-old trans male. He was assigned female at birth. Jalen has been on hormones since the age of 16. Prior to that, he was on GnRH (gonadotropin releasing hormones) puberty blockers. Jalen is in a relationship with a 28-year-old cisgender male. They plan to get married soon and then would like to start a family. Ideally, Jalen would like to carry their child.

Exploring clinical material

There are generally five ways to become a parent. The first is to have a child with another person, second is to foster a child, the third is to adopt a child (adoption may be part of the fostering process), fourth is to marry a person who has children of their own, and fifth is using a surrogate mother. In order to have a child with another person there needs to be a source for eggs and sperm, or genetic material. Trans people may need to consider whether or not becoming a parent is important to them, as some medical aspects of transition (e.g., hormones or surgery) may make having a child with their own genetic material difficult if not impossible. Hormone treatment can impact a person's ability to provide a gamete (e.g., mature egg or sperm). Without the presence of "opposite-sex" gametes it is impossible for humans to procreate. It is possible to reverse some of the changes that occur through hormone treatment by stopping the hormones for a period of time. People who were assigned female at birth may commence with a menstrual cycle. People who were assigned male at birth may see an increase in their sperm count. What complicates stopping of hormones is that some of the changes that occur are attributes that were causing the trans person distress prior to transition. It will be important to explore this with your client to ensure they are prepared for the types of challenges that may arise.

If, as in the case of Jalen, a person began their gender transition during adolescence (or childhood) and initiated GnRH treatment, it is highly likely this person will be unable to provide mature genetic material. Gametes complete the maturation process when a person is going through puberty. Since GnRH treatments block puberty, eggs or sperm may not mature. Puberty can start for some people as young as nine years old. It may be hard for a child this young to know whether they want to be a parent later in life. However, the decision to initiate puberty blockers may effectively foreclose options for becoming a parent. If a trans person initiated medical treatment for the purpose of blocking puberty, it is unlikely they will want to stop the blockers (or hormones as in Jalen's case) to commence an endogenous puberty. This can be a source of grief if the trans person wanted to become a parent. This type of grief may not be familiar for counselors, yet it can be devastating for a person. In addition to the grief a person experiences, they may also feel as though the provider who initiated puberty blockers did not give them all of the information about how blockers would impact parenting.

For adults (or people who have already completed puberty), it is possible to preserve their gametes for future use. The medical technology exists to preserve eggs; however, eggs are much more fragile than are sperm. Even though a person may be able to preserve their eggs, they may or may not be viable at a later time. In addition to this, the preservation of eggs is significantly more expensive than is the preservation of sperm.

Adoption and fostering

An alternative that has been available for a long period of time is adoption. Adoption can be of a U.S.- or a foreign-born child. The ability to adopt may be hampered by the laws in the state in which a person plans to adopt. At the time of this writing, 25 states and 2 territories have specific protection regarding discrimination based on sexual orientation or gender identity for people who would like to adopt. Eleven states allow state-licensed child welfare agencies to refuse placement with an LGBTQ+ family (Movement Advancement Project 2020). The same is true for who can foster a child. Sadly, there are LGBTQ+ people who would make excellent parents and there is a clear need for more foster or adoptive homes, but laws in some states prevent fostering or adoption.

If a trans person already has a child(ren) prior to entering a relationship, they can petition for stepparent adoption in any state in the U.S., provided that their relationship (marriage) is recognized by the state. This is available in part due to the 2015 U.S. Supreme Court ruling that led to marriage equality (*Obergefell et al. v. Hodges* 2015). The same is true when a same-sex couple has a child; the parent who did not provide genetic material can achieve parent status through second-parent adoption.

When considering the case of Jalen, the only choices he may have are becoming a foster or adoptive parent. This may be a disappointment for Jalen, but if neither Jalen's parents nor his providers had a conversation about this when he initiated GnRH, he likely did not realize that he would be in this place. Helping Jalen to work through the grief that may come up will be important. As a part of the grief process, ensuring Jalen understands some of the other options for becoming a parent may help to shorten the grief or lessen the pain.

EXPERT COMMENT

Jalen is part of a new generation of trans men who had access to puberty blockers prior to starting on testosterone. This means Jalen has less need to seek surgical treatment to reduce the impact of secondary sex characteristics that occur during a feminizing puberty. Although this is a large benefit, it also moves decisions about having genetically related children to an early age.

In therapy, Jalen may need support to manage grief, loss, regret, resentment, and anger about his past, present, and future. The loss of informed consent as a young person means that his opportunity to consider choices about having genetically related children was taken from him. Jalen may struggle with having a body that cannot provide the options he wants for family building. He may worry about not feeling bonded or feeling separate from a child he adopts or fosters and may experience family, friends, and community valuing biological parenthood over other family building options (Chen et al. 2019).

When offering support or information to Jalen about family building alternatives, the ultimate focus should be empowering Jalen to make the right decisions for himself (dickey, Ducheny, and Ehrbar 2016). Although he may be unlikely to select the option of halting his hormone therapy and going through an endogenous puberty in an attempt to produce mature eggs and carry a pregnancy, the decision is his. He may experience sadness, anger, guilt, and resentment at having to make such a difficult, forced choice, and he will have to carefully weigh the profound impact this will have on his life, body, and mental health.

Another option Jalen and his partner could consider is a surrogate pregnancy using his partner's sperm. The surrogate would provide the egg and uterus to carry the pregnancy and Jalen's partner would provide the sperm. Jalen could then adopt the baby. Many family and parenting constellations exist in trans and non-binary people's lives. It will be important to clarify the relationship of the surrogate with the child and whether the surrogate will be involved in co-parenting before beginning the process. Jalen can also explore the option of fostering or adopting a child. Jalen may need support in managing a belief that these options are "less than" carrying the pregnancy himself and in knowing that fostering a child may not ultimately result in adoption and permanent family building. Although adoption/fostering is legal for trans people in many places, it can still be difficult, and Jalen should be encouraged to pursue trans-friendly adoption and fostering agencies.

Jalen could also explore whether he is interested in chest feeding an infant (dickey, Ducheny, and Ehrbar 2016). He may feel that this offers him an intimate connection with his child. No matter what option(s) Jalen chooses, he may experience feelings of loss threaded through his joy of having a child and starting a family. Helping Jalen hold both while still immersing himself in the happiness of family building will offer support. Helping Jalen connect to other trans parents who have made some similar family building choices could help Jalen and his partner find a supportive and aware community.

Expert comment authored by Kelly Ducheny, PsyD, Chicago, IL

Take-home messages

Having age-appropriate discussions with your clients about parenting will help to avoid a situation in which your client would like to be a parent and they come to realize they have foreclosed on that option based on their medical transition. As stated in the chapter, the younger the child begins puberty blockers the less likely they are to fully understand their desire to be a parent. Jalen was 16 years old when he began taking hormones, but no one talked to him about wanting to be a parent. In hindsight, he is not sure what he would have thought about parenting. Helping your clients navigate the options for being an adoptive or foster parent may be a part of your work.

CHAPTER 13

Intersecting Identities

There is little doubt that trans and non-binary people face challenges simply because of their gender identity. This becomes complicated when a trans person also has an intersecting identity that represents a marginalized group (e.g., race or ethnicity, disability, socioeconomic status, sexual orientation, immigration status). The concept of intersectionality has been attributed to Kimberlé Crenshaw (1991). Crenshaw first proposed intersectionality as she recognized the myriad ways Black women were mistreated. In Crenshaw's work, sex and race were the intersecting identities and the concern was sexual violence.

Crenshaw explores the ways "in which race and gender intersect in shaping structural, political, and representational aspects of violence against women of color" (Crenshaw 1991, p.1244). Crenshaw explains structural intersectionality by describing the ways that women who immigrate to the U.S. often have to choose between the risk of being deported or staying with an abusive partner. This same situation could easily be true for trans women of color. Another example of structural intersectionality relates to the requirement for men to register for the selective service. Anyone who was assigned male at birth is required to register for the selective service within 30 days of their 18th birthday. A person may not be eligible for a job or student loans if they have not registered for the selective service, and this can have a significant impact for a trans person living in poverty. Arguably, people who are living in poverty need access to employment or support to attend school. Yet, trans people may not be able to access that support. It is possible to apply for a Status Information Letter (SIL) that indicates you are not eligible for the selective service. The NCTE (2020b) remarks that the SIL only states that you are not eligible to register for the selective service and not the reason for being ineligible. As such, a trans person does not out themselves by offering the letter to a prospective employer or office of financial aid.

Political intersectionality (Crenshaw 1991) refers to the ways a person is forced to choose between identities when attempting to fight for their rights. Using trans women of color as an example, we know they have the highest rates of HIV infection in the U.S. (James et al. 2016) There are several reasons why this might be the case. The fact that many trans women of color end up being homeless, which may lead to engaging in street economies, such as sex work, puts them at increased risk of sexual transmission of HIV. The political fights here are for decriminalizing sex work and ensuring trans women of color are eligible for care under programs such as the Ryan White HIV/AIDS program through the U.S. Department of Health and Human Services (2019). In 2014, the World Health Organization called for the decriminalization of drug use and sex work as a means of reducing the rates of HIV infection (NCTE 2014).

Representational intersectionality (Crenshaw 1991), as it applies to trans people, might include the representation of trans women in pornography as "she-males." Representation, in this way, includes misogyny and possibly racism, depending on who is being portrayed in the pornographic material. The use of the term "she-males" is derogatory. When using "she-male" in this type of material, people can easily make the assumption that "she-male" is an acceptable term. Although it is unlikely that trans allies will use this term, some people feel entitled to use terms like "she-male" or "tranny." This is an example of one of the ways that trans people experience microaggressions (Nadal 2013). When microaggressions accumulate, the damage to the individual is significant.

Details of the case

Phoebe is a 42-year-old African American trans woman. Phoebe is unemployed and has a disability but has yet to receive a favorable determination from the Social Security Administration. Phoebe first applied for disability two years ago. She experiences chronic pain due to the injuries she sustained when she was assaulted by a police officer.

There was no video of the assault and the officer has denied having assaulted Phoebe. As a result, there has been no recourse and Phoebe has over $20,000 in medical debt that she cannot afford to repay. Phoebe also has a significant trauma history due to the assault and to the abusive experiences she had in childhood.

Exploring clinical material

You have been seeing Phoebe for one month. You work in a community mental health agency. When Phoebe completed her intake paperwork, she indicated having been referred to your agency by a member of a street outreach program with whom you collaborate. Phoebe reports that she uses the pronouns she/her/hers. She also states that she has been using hormones that she gets from a friend. She is unsure where her friend gets the hormones and as long as her friend is able to share them, Phoebe does not feel comfortable inquiring as to their origin.

Your agency recently began a collaboration with an LGBTQ health center in the area. You make a referral for Phoebe. Two weeks later in your session, Phoebe admits she has not been able to secure an appointment at the health center. They require identity documents Phoebe does not currently have. She has a state identification, but she does not have her birth certificate. Phoebe thinks her parents may have her birth certificate, but she has not had contact with them for several years and has little interest in reaching out to them. You are concerned about the source of Phoebe's hormones and you ask her if you could help arrange an appointment for her. You have worked with some of the staff at the health center and are hopeful that you will be able to secure an appointment.

Phoebe admits that she no longer has a place to live. She feels like she has exhausted all of the resources she has of friends who live in the area. When asked what she has been doing in the evenings, she states she has been engaging in survival sex. She has found some people who seem willing to take her in for the evening and offer her a meal and a place to sleep in exchange for sex. As the two of you talk about this you realize Phoebe is feeling hopeless about her situation.

You have had a hard time getting Phoebe to talk about her history of trauma. She very quickly closes down as you begin to explore her trauma history. Without ever having asked Phoebe the questions from the Adverse Childhood Experiences checklist (Dube et al. 2001), you are certain she has experienced at least eight of the adverse childhood experiences. In passing, Phoebe has mentioned the mistreatment she experienced from her father in childhood. To this point, all you know is that her father "punished me for acting like a girl" beginning at a young age.

Although Phoebe has a trauma history, she is also a very resilient person. Resilience, or the ability to bounce back from a difficult situation, is an important psychological concept that merits clinical focus. Southwick et al. (2014) discuss the various aspects of resilience. This includes an understanding that resilience exists on a spectrum and varies across the lifespan, and that context plays a critical role in one's ability to be resilient.

In one of the first studies to explore resilience in trans people, Singh et al. (2011) found five common themes and two variant themes. The common themes are: "(a) evolving a self-generated definition of self, (b) embracing self-worth, (c) awareness of oppression, (d) connection with a supportive community, and (e) cultivating hope for the future" (Singh et al. 2011, p.23). The variant themes were social activism and being positive role models for others. It will be useful to work with Phoebe in helping her place herself within these themes of resilience. Even if she is only able to understand her self-worth, this should help the ways in which she shows up in the world and may help her to find the strength to work through life's challenges.

EXPERT COMMENT

Phoebe's situation highlights the importance of understanding the full complexity of the human experience. Clinicians cannot understand her story without understanding American racism—both in day-to-day life and in the form of "baked in" disparities in institutional responses. But this is not all. Among other things, she is also impacted by her poverty, the criminalization of sex work, and intersecting all of this, her trans identity. None of these factors stands alone or apart from the others in how Phoebe experiences life or in how others respond to her. Finally, both barriers to meeting her practical needs and potential sources of resiliency depend on understanding cultural and community values for the many communities of which Phoebe is a member.

The clinician must also learn, with her, legal requirements having to do with her disability application, her birth certificate, and other issues, and how all of these interface with her physical and mental health challenges, her trauma history, and of course, her trans identity. Clinicians may find themselves lacking personal experience with some, many, or even all of the various layers of an experience like Phoebe's. There may be nothing wrong with this. The answer is not always to find Phoebe a clinician who is "just like her" (whatever that means). We must *all* hone our intersectional thinking. This is an *extension* of Crenshaw's work but a *necessary* one—Crenshaw studied the experiences of African American women, and Phoebe *is* an African American woman. No explanation excluding her would be complete. But intersectionality is not just how Phoebe sees life but also how others see Phoebe. With these multiple identities come multiple roles for the clinician.

As this chapter moves from general policies to issues specific to Phoebe, the clinician must think and act as a therapist/psychologist, as an ally, but also in many ways as a support coordinator or caseworker. Importantly, the therapist is also a learner and a collaborator. This is an eclectic mixture of skills! Clinicians will often need to do "homework" themselves, to help their patients navigate complex policies. The clinician can use advantages of their formal training as well as life-long learning of "the way things work." If the clinician has not faced the kinds of barriers Phoebe has faced, they should turn this into an advantage— the clinician and patient can achieve something in collaboration that neither could achieve alone.

Phoebe is also a teacher. She is the expert in the room on herself. As clinicians start to experience her life with her, they must resist overly simplistic stereotypes. They must be honest about their own intersecting biases about many different aspects of her experience. Finally, they must explore their own process in balancing competing demands. Harm-reduction models are often critical to success, but clinicians must constantly balance their bias toward rigid adherence to "gold standards" of care against any tendency to sell marginalized individuals short based on erroneous assumptions about what they can or cannot achieve.

Expert comment authored by Mira Jourdan, PhD, ABPP, Grand Rapids, MI

Take-home messages

There are several messages that we can take from understanding Phoebe's case. The first is the importance of using a trauma-informed approach to work with trans and gender non-binary clients (Richmond, Burnes, and Carroll 2012; Richmond et al. 2017). Second is the importance of using a harm-reduction model of care. Harm-reduction models of care with trans and gender non-binary people would allow the trans client to continue taking hormones while the client worked to become an established patient with a provider who would be able to follow the client's hormone treatment (Coleman et al. 2011; Dietz and Halem 2016).

A final take-home message from this chapter is a reminder of the ways that a person's intersecting (marginalized) identities can quickly complicate an everyday experience that is often filled with mistreatment, discrimination, and violence. Clients need to be able to unpack these challenges in a way that means they can begin to marshal their resources with an eye toward resilience and self-worth.

CHAPTER 14

Military Service Members and Veterans

S erving in the military for one's country is an act of civil engagement that signals a strong commitment to the health, safety, and well-being of citizens. Regardless of the branch of the military in which a person serves, members of the military make significant sacrifices. In this chapter, I explore some of the challenges that trans military service members face. Trans people, whether they are active duty, in the reserves, have retired, or have left the military in some other way may have clinical needs they do not want to bring to military or Veterans Administration (VA) providers. Civilian providers should be prepared to see these individuals as it relates to military service, mood disorders (or other clinical material), or their gender identity as I focus on in this case.

Trans and gender non-binary people have long been over-represented in the U.S. military (Gates and Herman 2014; Shipherd, Mizock, Maguen, and Green 2012). Gates and Herman (2014) and NCTE and partners (n.d.) both state that trans people serve in the military at twice the rate of the general public. Shipherd and colleagues (2012) explored the rates at which trans people who were assigned male at birth served in the military. They found the rates in their sample to be three times higher than the general population.

In this chapter, I explore the experience of a military service member. What has made life confusing is that in 2016 the military changed their policy thereby allowing trans people to serve openly in the military. In 2019, President Trump announced that the policy would be rescinded and the ban on trans people serving in the military would be back in place (NCTE et al. n.d.). This new regulation created exempt and non-exempt classifications for trans military service members (Norquist 2019). As long as a service member had a diagnosis of gender dysphoria by April 11, 2019, they would be able to access care and serve openly. Service members who are non-exempt are allowed to identify as trans, but they must serve in the sex they were assigned at birth. Additionally, non-exempt service members are not eligible for transition-related medical care. If a provider determines that transition-related care is medically necessary, the service member is at risk of being involuntarily separated from the service. This puts the lives and livelihood of trans military service members at risk. Trans people who have come out to their command may now be at risk of losing their standing with the U.S. military or of being victimized by members of their unit or their command.

Details of the case

DeShawn is a 26-year-old African American who was assigned male at birth. DeShawn has been in the U.S. Army for eight years having enlisted after high school graduation. DeShawn is a staff sergeant. When DeShawn is alone, usually in a motel, he dresses in women's clothing and refers to himself as Shanice. DeShawn is afraid to come out to any of his fellow soldiers for fear they will not be accepting and he will get hurt. DeShawn has yet to use an affirmed name or pronouns that are consistent with their[6] gender identity.

Exploring clinical material

You are a mental health provider and have an office that is near to the base where DeShawn is stationed. You are listed on several online databases as being competent in work with transsexual, transgender, and cross-dressing people. You have noticed on your caller ID that someone has called several times but has failed to leave a message. You are beginning to think it is a spam call or a robo-caller. Finally, you receive a message from DeShawn. He states he would like to come see you but needs to know more about the location where you work, as he is worried others will see him enter your office. You assure him your office is discretely located in a professional building with many other types of professionals (e.g., accountants, attorneys, medical providers). Also, you have a private waiting area and your office is marked with only the unit number.

DeShawn comes to the first appointment and he has completed the paperwork, which he downloaded from your web site. As you are reading through the information provided you see that he did not check the boxes for sex or for marital status. When you ask about that, DeShawn's face gives away his true feelings and he says, "I left them blank because the way the questions are asked, they do not apply to me." You get the unmistakable feeling that your paperwork has one or more insensitive questions. You ask DeShawn what would fit better. He explains he usually wishes people would not even bother collecting this type of information. He says, "It is mostly unimportant and does not really tell you anything about why I came to see you." You agree with that thought and then talk for just a bit about how insurance companies and other third-party payers often ask, especially for the sex of the client. You tell DeShawn you will work with some of your colleagues to develop a new intake form that addresses his concerns.

At this point, you know that the rest of the session will make or break your work with DeShawn. You introduce yourself again and this time you include your pronouns. After finishing your typical verbal informed consent, you ask DeShawn what pronouns to use and what brings him to counseling. DeShawn states that at this time he is still using male pronouns. He goes on to give a little bit of history about the ways he experiences depression and anxiety. For the next several weeks you work with DeShawn to understand his anxiety and depression symptoms and to help him to develop some coping skills such as the use of a thought record. The underlying theme of the irrational thoughts has to do with low self-esteem and feelings of hopelessness. After DeShawn has mastered these skills, your work is terminated since you had met the clinical goals.

About ten months later you receive a voice mail message from DeShawn. He sounds distressed and asks that you call him back during a very specific time period. He does not explain why he has such a short window to connect, but you do your best to ensure you have at least ten minutes during that time. Consider the following conversation.

DeShawn: Thank you so much for calling me back. I am scared and do not know what to do.

Counselor: I only have about ten minutes right now, and I am glad you called. It sounds like something difficult has happened to you.

DeShawn: They found out. I have been hiding this for so long, but they found out. [DeShawn is weeping and is clearly distraught.]

Counselor: Take a deep breath DeShawn. Try to slow down if you can. Who are "they"?

DeShawn: My commander. I feel like they set me up.

Counselor: I am really lost, DeShawn. What is this about?

DeShawn: Oh no, I have to go. [DeShawn quickly hangs up.]

You attempt to call DeShawn back but the number you were given does not have voice mail. You are concerned for DeShawn, but you have no other way of reaching out to him. As you think about the short conversation, you realize he did not say anything that indicates he is a danger to himself or anyone else, at least not directly. Several days later you receive another call from DeShawn. He asks if he can come see you for the first available appointment. You schedule him later that same day.

When DeShawn comes into your office, you can see he has been crying. You gently ask him what has happened. After taking several deep breaths, he explains he has been discharged from the Army. You give DeShawn the space to tell the story. He states he did not realize people had been following him. He tells you he has been leading a secret life. DeShawn also states he would like to be referred to with female pronouns and by the name Shanice. She says, "As long as I have to figure out how to live my life outside of the Army I might as well be able to be myself." This is the first real indication you have that Shanice identifies as a trans person. You summarize what you have heard from Shanice so far to be sure you understand what has been happening.

As you work with Shanice, you realize in addition to being discharged from the Army, she has also been disowned by her family. She states she has contact with one cousin but everyone else (e.g., parents, siblings, grandparents) "wants nothing to do with me." You work with Shanice as you begin to understand her goals for transition. At this time, she states she simply wants to present as female. She is unsure about plans to make a medical transition mostly due to the cost. You offer to Shanice that if she wants, she can come to a session dressed as female. She states she is worried about walking into the office building dressed as female. You offer that she is more than welcome to bring her clothes in with her and she can change in the restroom. You show her where the restroom is and assure her it is an all-gender restroom and she will be safe changing her clothing there. In subsequent sessions she comes in dressed in an affirming way. You continue to work with her as she explores her identity and gets back on her feet.

EXPERT COMMENT

Shanice's case is a realistic example of how a civilian provider might encounter a transgender service member as a patient in the community. Due to the risk of being involuntarily discharged, transgender service members may intentionally seek care outside of the Military Healthcare System (MHS). As such, community providers specializing in transgender care should be prepared to work with service members and veterans, even if they are not Department of Defense (DoD) or Veterans Health Administration (VHA) employees.

As illustrated in the case example, transgender service members may be fearful of seeking care and mistrustful of mental health providers. When working with this population it is important to understand how service members' lived experiences of institutionalized discrimination may impact their presentation when attempting to access care (Chen et al. 2017; Eleazer 2016). Military policies have historically provided several tools (such as Don't Ask, Don't Tell; appearance and grooming regulations; criminal charges; non-judicial punishment) for forcing transgender persons out of military service (Kerrigan 2012). However, military medical regulations have been the primary mechanism used to involuntarily discharge transgender service members (Eleazer 2019; Norquist 2019). As such, military medical and mental health providers have played a critical role in the implementation of these discriminatory policies (Dietert and Dentice 2015; Eleazer 2016; Parco,

Levy, and Spears 2015). As a result, transgender service members may seek care for presenting problems connected to their experiences as a transgender person (e.g., relational problems, depressed mood, posttraumatic stress) without disclosing their gender identity or symptoms of gender dysphoria. Never forget that your office may be the only space where your patient feels safe to be their authentic self and that providing an affirming therapeutic relationship can be an incredibly powerful intervention.

Frequent policy changes and legal challenges have resulted in uncertainty among service members, unit leadership, and providers (Eleazer 2019). As part of an ongoing informed consent process, community providers should discuss with patients how an evolving policy context may impact confidentiality, billing, and the risks of treatment. For example, billing a service member's military insurance for gender dysphoria may out them to military leaders and cause them to be discharged. Stay informed about policy changes and seek consultation as needed so that you and your patient can work together to make the best decisions about their care.

Continually assess for any changes in your patient's military status that might impact risk and patient care, particularly if a service member becomes subject to investigation or is involuntarily discharged. For example, in Shanice's case, being discharged will likely impact her financial stability and access to health insurance coverage. Involuntary discharges are often completed as quickly as possible, without allowing sufficient time for the service member to find civilian employment or prepare for the abrupt loss of income, healthcare, and access to base housing. Providers working with recently discharged veterans might consider reassessing the client's eligibility for pro-bono or sliding-scale services.

Even in ideal circumstances, transitioning out of military service can impact psychosocial functioning across several domains. For many troops, being a soldier, sailor, airman, or marine is a central part of their identity. Military service is more than just a job and most service members work, eat, sleep, and engage in recreation almost exclusively on military installations. Military units foster a sense of family among members and provide close social connection and support. For Shanice, her abrupt loss of military community is compounded by a lack of affirming family support. Sadly, this experience is not uncommon and many transgender service members suffer rejection from family members, friends, religious communities, and other non-military support systems as they are simultaneously losing connection to their military community. One of the most important things providers can do to reduce suicide risk and support clients transitioning to civilian life is to connect them with gender-affirming social supports (Carter et al. 2019) (see resources listed in Appendix C).

After leaving the military, Shanice may become eligible for VA healthcare benefits and may prefer to transition her mental healthcare to the VA. Currently, the VA does not cover gender-affirming surgical procedures. However, VHA offers several gender-affirming treatments for qualified veterans such as surgery referral letters, pre- and post-operative care, psychotherapy, hormone therapy, hair removal, and prosthetics (including wigs, vaginal dilators, packers, stand-to-pee devices, binders, and gaffes). However, many transgender veterans avoid seeking care at the VA or disclosing their gender identity to VA providers (James et al. 2016). Qualification criteria for VA healthcare and benefits can be complex, and transgender veterans may make inaccurate assumptions about their eligibility, causing them to miss out on valuable services and benefits that they have earned (e.g., healthcare, supported housing, vocational training and support, higher education). As such, it is important to initiate conversations with veterans about their engagement with VA services. You might also consider forging a connection with the LGBTQ+ Veteran Care Coordinator at your local VA medical center for consultation and referrals.

Expert comment authored by Jacob Eleazer, PhD, New Haven, CT, and Landon Marchant, BA, Williamstown, MA

Take-home messages

Two ideas are important to take away from Shanice's story. The first is that it is so important to have paperwork that is affirming of trans people's identities. This may require you to review your paperwork every 6–12 months. Language used by trans people can change quickly. Although it is easier to have pre-selected choices for gender, sexuality, and other demographic details, trans people are likely to appreciate the use of open-ended answer options. If there is a need to capture a person's sex (e.g., for insurance purposes), this can easily be asked of the client in the intake session after explaining the need for the information. If you are using an electronic health record you may not be able to change the answer choices in the record. However, it is worth the effort to reach out to the company to ask them to update their answer choices to include (a) sex assigned at birth and (b) gender identity. Trans people are likely to feel seen in these question options. Cisgender people may be a bit confused as to why you are asking two questions that seem to be asking the same thing, but when they look at the answer choices the confusion should quickly dissipate.

The second take-home message is about having a space that will allow your trans clients to change their clothes before their session. As we saw in the case of Shanice, the provider not only had an all-gender restroom but also made the time to show Shanice how to access the restroom prior to a session. This may not feel like a perfect solution for your clients. However, by providing an all-gender restroom, your clients have not only a safe place to change their clothing before a session but also a safe place to use the restroom. Restrooms, especially public restrooms, can be unsafe for trans people. It is a place where some trans people can be policed by others, often putting the trans person at risk of injury.

CHAPTER 15

Coming Out to Your Children

In some cases, transgender people need to come out to their family, including minor or adult children. This case will explore the differences in response that children might have based on the age that they learn about their parent's gender identity. Generally speaking, unless a child is in puberty, they will be relatively supportive of their parent's transition. We also address possible difficulties faced when the other parent is unsupportive.

Details of the case
Alicia is a 44-year-old trans woman. She was assigned male at birth. She identifies as Latina. Alicia was married to her high school sweetheart for 20 years. Together, she and her wife have three children. The children are Alex (age 19), Anna (age 16), and Adam (age 11). Alicia and Amber (her wife) divorced two years ago in large part due to Alicia's decision to make a medical transition.

Exploring clinical material
You have been working with Alicia for five years. Although she is very confident about her gender identity, she and Amber have not been able to resolve their differences about coming out to the children. Alicia wants to come out to them, and Amber is adamantly opposed to the idea. Shortly after coming out to Amber, Alicia moved out of the family home into an apartment nearby. She spends as much time as possible with the children but "always on their turf." Being on their turf means she always dresses as a male, per

Amber's request. The same is true about her place of work—Alicia dresses in traditionally male attire.

Alicia is ready to come out to others but is not sure how to go about that. She wants to start with her children, as her family is the most important aspect of her life. You start by asking her what she thinks will happen if she tells the children. She begins to get tearful as she says Amber will file for sole custody, claiming that Alicia is unfit as a parent, and ask for a judgment that Alicia not be able to see the children. "The best I can hope for," says Alicia, "is supervised visits." Alicia maintains that she will have to be dressed as "a man" for those visits to happen. It is clear to you that this is not an option Alicia wants to consider.

It is not uncommon for there to be a disagreement between parents about how and when to talk to children about plans for a transition, whether social or medical. Further, some spouses will use a person's transition against them (as Amber is doing) by creating personal and legal obstacles to being with the children. Personal obstacles include what Alicia is facing now. Amber will let Alicia see the children only in the family home and insists she dress in male attire. Legally, the worst-case scenario is that a custody case develops, and the end result is a ruling that makes it impossible for Alicia to see the children.

There is no evidence that a person's trans status makes them unfit for parenting. In fact, just the opposite has been the case in the research literature (White and Ettner 2004, 2007). To the extent that there is support for the trans spouse from the cisgender spouse, it is more likely the children will see this in much the same way as they see other changes in the family dynamic. For example, one parent may have stayed at home until the children were all in school. Once they were all in school, that parent got a job. This will create a new dynamic in the household and is likely to be disruptive. Although making a social or medical transition is different on many levels, having support from the other spouse makes a big difference in terms of the children being resilient.

Alicia, to this point, has made a social transition in only a few places in her life, including your office. When she arrives at your office she is usually coming from work. She wants to be able to fully express herself with you; however, she does not know how to do that. You have been using the name Alicia with her for some time now. You suggest that if Alicia wants to, she could change her clothes in the "family" restroom prior to the session. She arrives early to the following session and takes a change of clothes into the "family" restroom. She changes into what she calls her "Alicia clothes" and then proceeds to the waiting room.

As you begin the session you comment on Alicia's attire. Although this is not something you would normally do, it feels important since this is the first time you have seen Alicia dressed this way. She is a bit self-conscious. She admits this is the third or fourth time she has worn women's clothing outside of her apartment. Consider this conversation:

Counselor: How does it feel to express yourself as a woman here with me?

Alicia: It feels good. I feel a little bit uncomfortable, just because I've done this only a few times. I'm glad that I did it though.

Counselor: Say more about that.

Alicia: You know I wear women's clothes at home, and I've wanted to wear them in public. I'm grateful that you've been so supportive and helped me be able to dress this way here with you.

Counselor: You are welcome, Alicia. I can imagine this was challenging even though you are glad you were able to change clothes before our session.

Alicia: Well, let's just say that my morning routine was pretty different as I had to pack things up before I left for work. I didn't sleep very well last night because I kept thinking of things I needed to remember. It was almost like taking a trip somewhere, even though I just had a single change of clothing.

There is plenty to explore with Alicia in this session, including the difficulty sleeping. It is good to spend time reflecting on her decision to change clothes before the session. If you had chosen not to say anything, it may have led to a rupture in the clinical relationship. Imagine being in her shoes and taking a risk with someone you know. They do not say a word about your effort. Understandably, you might feel hurt. The same may have been true for Alicia. Further, she may not feel safe asking you why you did not say something. Part of this is due to the power imbalance inherent in mental health work. The other piece may be related to a concern that she has dressed in a way that is not acceptable. Both of these reasons can lead to a significant issue in your work with Alicia.

Two weeks later, Alicia arrives at your office and is clearly distraught. She reports having just learned that Amber hired a private detective. This person has been following Alicia around, unbeknownst to her. Amber forwarded a photo of her walking out of your office two weeks ago, the week she first dressed as Alicia. Alicia reports that Amber plans to report this to the judge and ask for permanent, sole custody. Additionally, she will ask that any visits Alicia is allowed—"if I am allowed visits"—be supervised by Child Protective Services.

After listening to Alicia, you lead her through a mindfulness exercise to help bring her into the present. Your conversation following the exercise goes like this:

Counselor: I can see that you are upset by this Alicia. Are you feeling a bit more centered after that exercise?

Alicia: Yes, thank you, that is helping. I just don't understand how angry she has become.

Counselor: I can understand how you might be confused. Until you came out to Amber, you always thought of her as your best friend, your confidante. Now, it seems like you can't count on her for anything. Am I understanding that correctly?

Alicia: Yes. She's been very unpredictable, and now this stupid private detective. I feel betrayed by her.

Counselor: I can see how you would feel that way. Didn't she say the same thing to you when you came out to her? That she felt betrayed by you? [*Note:* You have been working with Alicia for five years. Even though this question may feel like you are siding with Amber, you feel certain that in your work with Alicia that she will not feel unsupported.]

Alicia: Yes, but this feels different.

Counselor: How so?

Alicia: I feel violated by that. I just don't understand how my identity makes me a bad parent. I don't act any differently with my children. And, they tell me how much they love and miss me. They don't understand why I left the house. That's the hardest part for me and is why I want to come out to the children.

Counselor: So they will understand?

Alicia: Yes, and so they don't have to make up stories about what is going on. I can only imagine what Amber might be saying to them. I try not to spend too much time thinking about that.

Counselor: Remind yourself that no matter what Amber says, your life matters. You are a strong, beautiful person—inside and out. I know it can be easy to forget that when it feels like all you hear are negative comments.

Alicia: Thanks, I need that reminder.

It is reasonable to expect that Alicia will experience ups and downs as she navigates coming out and her previous marriage. It may be appropriate to refer Alicia to a peer-led support group. Being with others who have had similar experiences may help her to gain more insight about how to respond.

Over a period of time, Alicia is able to come out to her children. Amber remains angry about this, but Alicia wants to be able to see her children and be herself. The children have some questions about how to refer to Alicia. She says it would be okay for them to call her Dad in private, but in public she wants them to call her Alicia. She is clear about knowing she is not their mother in the ways that Amber is, and she thought it would be best for everyone if the children called her Alicia.

As stated earlier, children are usually pretty flexible when it comes to learning about a parent's decision to transition. The time when this is least likely to be the case is if the child is in the throes of puberty. Given the questions an adolescent might be having about their own body and the changes they are experiencing, it makes sense they may feel overwhelmed on learning about a parent's gender identity.

EXPERT COMMENT

Numerous challenges can arise when a trans person is in a relationship and has children. These issues are not insurmountable, but they take a great deal of care. Mental health providers are encouraged to be mindful of any tension that might exist in a trans person's relationship. Addressing the partner's concern may require clinical finesse, but the partner's concerns are no less important than those of the trans person.

Transgender individuals often postpone transitioning due to the anticipated pain and suffering they believe it will cause their families. The foreboding realization that the relationships they are trying to protect with their parents, partners, and children are often the ones in which they will experience the deepest and most tremendous amount of pain can be devastating, isolating, and immobilizing. Partners and children can be two of the most vulnerable relationships during a transition, and unfortunately, loss is far too common of an outcome. Partners may feel betrayed and devalued, thereby becoming incensed at having lost the person they planned to spend their golden years with, enjoying grandchildren together. Transgender women's parental rights are routinely reduced to supervised visits or eliminated completely by judges who are often uneducated or ill-informed about gender identity and positive parenting.

On the other hand, it is often those who love and support transgender individuals who help embolden them to step outside of society's gender roles and move forward in becoming the person on the outside they truly feel they are on the inside. Children of transgender individuals are often one such source of support that propels transgender individuals to live authentically, and sometimes those are the relationships most likely to be strengthened. Children are easily and routinely shaped by society and the actions of their role models. But they can also be the driving force of change, propelling social justice movements and having a hand in reforming our societies.

Potential loss of support is quite often the reason transgender individuals chose to remain living a life of incongruence long after they have come to absolute terms with their true gender identity. Healthcare professionals can help offset these losses and the negative effects of social stigma that are still very prevalent in the Western world. Having an understanding therapist who recognizes the issues and cares enough to learn how to treat their transgender clients serves as a protective factor, can bolster the client's support system, and helps fill in where there is loss, making the transition more bearable. Past research supports that the more congruent a person is with their identity, the higher their level of well-being (Barr, Budge, and Adelson 2016; Glynn et al. 2016; Warren, Smalley, and Barefoot 2016). For counselors and therapists who value the humanistic knowledge shared by theorist and psychologist Carl Rogers, congruence is a known therapeutic factor, necessary for true health. Carl Rogers (1961) stated the curious paradox is that when a person accepts themselves, that is when they can change.

It has been my own personal experience that my child was and continues to be my main source of support, and our relationship has carried me through numerous times of self-doubt and discouragement. But not all outcomes are this positive, and as a counselor or therapist, helping transgender clients tread rough waters and navigate the ups and downs of their transition by being knowledgeable, supportive, and understanding may be one of the greatest gifts they can give to their clients.

Expert comment authored by Christopher Allen, PhD, Tulsa, OK

Take-home messages

Expecting the unexpected may be the most appropriate way to think about work with coming out among family members. It seemed that things were moving forward for Alicia and then her reaction to Amber's decision to hire a private detective changed the landscape.

Peer support has the potential to support your clients to build knowledge and skills that you may not be able to help with. Learning from your peers allows your client to have access to information that you may not ever be able to share because the information is either too personal for your role as a mental health provider or, if you are cisgender, you likely do not have that level of knowledge.

CHAPTER 16

Religious Values and Trans Identities

People who grow up in the U.S. are likely to attend a religious organization (e.g., Christian, Jewish, Buddhist, or Muslim to name a few). According to the Pew Research Center (2015), the number of people who claim a religious belief is decreasing. For example, the number of Christian believers dropped from 78.4 percent to 70.6 percent of the U.S. population from 2007 to 2014. At the same time, non-Christian faiths have seen an increase in believers.

Most people would agree that conservative religious faiths usually are not accepting of LGBTQ+ people. Although there have been changes in some mainstream religious organizations (e.g., Episcopalians, Lutherans, Unitarian Universalists), these changes may have come at a cost to LGBTQ+ people, some of whom were or are in the clergy. As an example, I was a member of a conservative Christian church in high school and college. When I came out as a lesbian it was made very clear that I had two choices. I could renounce my sexual orientation, and if I did I would be welcome in the church. Alternatively, even if I did not have a long-term relationship, if I acted even once on my same-sex attraction, I would be excommunicated from the church. This was all very confusing to me as a young adult. What made it especially confusing was that the person who I found myself attracted to was a woman whom I met through the church. Although our relationship was never sexual in nature, we had a very deep emotional bond. Even that was not acceptable in the eyes of church leaders.

Although the church I attended as a young adult still holds very conservative beliefs about who is and is not eligible for membership, there has been a significant change in other faith communities. Some denominations have developed discernment processes to determine whether their church is going to be open and affirming. This may involve a significant change to the rules of membership and can be a divisive process.

It can be very challenging for a person who has grown up in a specific faith tradition to come out if their faith community is not welcoming of LGBTQ+ people. In some cases, as we see in this chapter, family relationships may be severed due to a lack of acceptance and understanding.

Details of the case

Mark is a 58-year-old trans man. Mark grew up in Georgia and his father was a Baptist minister. Mark's father died about 17 years ago. His mother is currently living in a memory unit at a nursing home near his childhood home. Mark has not seen his mother since 1999. This was when Mark came out to his parents. He knew when he did that it would likely mean the end of his relationship with his parents. Mark has been sending money to the nursing home to help pay for some of his mother's care. He has not gone to visit her because he knows she probably will not recognize him, and even if she does, he will not be able to tolerate the use of the wrong name.

Exploring clinical material

You began working with Mark prior to his transition. He came to you after a difficult relationship breakup. Mark had been dating a woman he met in a 12-step group. Mark was devastated when their relationship ended as his partner dumped him for another person. This was the first time Mark experienced this type of relationship ending.

Mark isolated after the ending of his relationship. Outside of work and attending one 12-step meeting on a weekly basis, Mark rarely left the house. Over the next several months, Mark was debilitated by his depression. He took six weeks off work to help address his depression. Over time, Mark worked with his counselor to understand his part in his relationship history. Mark experienced three subsequent relationships that were shorter each time. As Mark explored his history, he continued to run into important religious values. He talked with his counselor about the tension that builds up for him when he thinks about the beliefs that were so important to him in adolescence and young adulthood. His heart tells him there is no way to have those beliefs and be a trans person. He realizes he has internalized the messages he heard from his parents and especially from his father. He has tried joining open and affirming churches, but he continually finds himself having an internal cringe moment when the minister begins reading from the bible or talking about Jesus.

Consider the following conversation:

Mark: I went to a different church this week.

Counselor: How was that for you?

Mark: It felt like more of the same. It seems that no matter which denomination I attend, there is always a strong message about Jesus.

Counselor: We have talked about how hard this is for you. I know this is connected to some of the messages you heard in high school and college about whether you would be welcome in a church community.

Mark: Yeah, it is as if those messages are stuck in my head and I always go back to the hateful comments that I, and other LGBTQ people, heard from church leaders. "You are going to burn in hell"; "You are a disgrace to the human race." The messages were so hateful that I finally left and in doing so lost the first real sense of family that I had experienced outside of my family of origin. [Mark begins to cry.]

Counselor: It seems this was more painful this time. What was different for you?

Mark: The church I went to had a guest speaker last week. I didn't realize that was going to happen. The guest speaker was the leader of the prayer group that I belonged to in college. I almost walked out when I saw him, but I decided to stay. In hindsight, I wish I had left.

For Mark, coming out as a trans man led him to completely disown his religious beliefs. He found a way to hold on to his values. For him, those values included honesty, curiosity, and loyalty. Even though he had no idea how he would move forward with a spiritual belief system, he knew that did not matter. What was important was that he live his life with integrity. It was when he came to that understanding that he finally found his voice to talk about his questions regarding his gender.

Mark's counselor was receptive to his desire to transition. However, she admitted she did not have the clinical experience to work with him in his transition. Mark's immediate reaction, which he did not share with his counselor, was that she was abandoning him. This was not the situation, but what Mark felt, as he moved forward to honor his gender, was that he was going to lose the important people in his life. There surely would be relationships that would not survive his transition, and what was important was that Mark honor what those relationships brought him and allow himself to experience grief.

Trans people are sometimes nervous to talk about grief. Historically, feelings of grief or loss were interpreted as being feelings of doubt. As such, it was an indication the trans person was not truly committed to making a transition. This is far from the truth as doubt and grief are not the same emotion. The grief is not limited to the trans person's experiences. Other members of the family system, even those who effectively disown their child, experience grief. Wahlig (2015) explored the ways that parents experience grief and loss when a child comes out as trans. Wahlig suggests that the grief and loss provide rich clinical material. The loss may be related to their expectations that the child would have a hetero- or gender-normative existence. She also states parental concern for the loss of religious support and the relationship they had with their child prior to coming out.

We all have deeply held values. For some of us, those values originated in the communities in which we were raised. For others the values may have come from a youth group (e.g., 4H, Girl Scouts). Making a decision to transition may involve consideration of whether and how one's values are consistent with one's identity. Mental health providers are encouraged to remain open to the feelings their trans and non-binary clients express. Left unaddressed, these feelings may continue to haunt the client in unnecessary ways.

EXPERT COMMENT

In the case of Mark, we observe a middle-aged trans man who is struggling with existential questions of belonging and acceptance in the context of his gender identity and psychic wounds. Mark's sense of self appears to be fractured as he struggles to integrate disparate external and internal messages that simultaneously affirm and negate his identity and value.

Mark engages in negative religious coping marked by a cynical worldview and continually conflicted relationships with God and others. Negative religious coping is associated with views that one is being divinely punished through adverse life events and that the Divine is powerless or unwilling to intervene on one's behalf. Negative religious coping methods do not provide a way to protect the person from the harmful effects of discrimination, hostility, and rejection that positive religious coping offers. Without an effective coping method, Mark has internalized the condemning and rejecting messages toward him from his parents, religious community, and multiple intimate partners resulting in his detachment from himself and from his entire system of meaning and belonging. This separation leaves Mark ungrounded and gives rise to his difficulties in emotional, physical, and spiritual self-care, demonstrated by Mark's patterns of avoidance, addictive behaviors, unmanageable internal distress, and inability to form or sustain meaningful relationships.

Mark operates from a rejecting schema through which he recreates his spiritual wounds and reinforces a distorted understanding of his self-worth and ability to belong. He appears to look for confirmation of his divine rejection and interprets any failure by others to meet his expectations as proof he is unacceptable and/or being punished. He thus unconsciously engages in re-enactments of being pushed outside the boundaries of support and acceptance by church, family, and partners and sets himself up for repeated experiences of abandonment.

The cycle of re-enactment exposes a conflict between hope and existential fear. Mark is stuck moving between spiritual promise and devastation. The contradictions of his belief that loyalty, integrity, and honesty are Christian values, but to be accepted he must choose to be dishonest and without integrity, leave Mark with an unbearable cognitive dissonance that he attempts to resolve by disowning his faith, family, and others. Challenging Mark's dichotomous thinking that he must abandon his beliefs to be himself necessitates exploring his religious and spiritual history.

It is necessary that the clinician do some exploration with Mark about the general beliefs of the religious tradition he was raised in to gain insights into his understanding of authority, punishment, divine intervention, human nature, guilt, obedience, and forgiveness. His religious upbringing will influence his understanding of intimate relationships and morality. This will in turn have a significant effect on how Mark processes the grief he feels about lost friendships and romantic relationships and whether, for example, these losses are divine punishment for sexual impurity, or whether he has a right to ask for help or be forgiven.

For Mark to work through his grief around relationship losses requires that his treatment address the larger loss of his relationship with a divine other and his religious and spiritual community that are intertwined with his gender affirmation. Mark describes traumatic stress responses and avoidance of what appear to be the symbols of his divine abandonment and punishment: the name Jesus, Bible readings, and his former name. Each triggers his grief over losses due to affirming his gender and reinforces his rejecting schema. Examining what Mark remembers and feels when he hears these references provides insight into the role of Mark's protective pattern of avoidance of discomfort. This may also be a way to understand Mark's relational patterns where he may habitually hide or close off parts of himself to a significant other to avoid negative judgment. Mark may re-enact disowning his beliefs in order to be himself by disowning his partners whenever he feels the demands of a relationship require him to change any aspect of himself. Without exploring these triggers, Mark may be unable to progress in changing his behavioral patterns in relationships and his self-sabotaging actions and may be unable to resolve his spiritual pain.

Expert comment authored by Ruben Hopwood, MDiv, PhD, Boston, MA

Take-home messages

Mark's experience is not unique. When the concern is related to reconciling religious beliefs and values, we must create a safe space for our clients. Without that space, trans and non-binary people may find themselves wallowing in emotional states they feel helpless to resolve.

In Mark's case, he needed to reconcile the conservative religious beliefs and values that were tied to his childhood experiences to his identity as a trans person. One aspect of that decision led to the loss of a connection with his parents. Even though Mark's father died many years ago, it is likely that Mark has unresolved concerns that will stay that way. This may also be true of his relationship with his mother. She is still alive, but her symptoms of dementia make it impossible for Mark to address unresolved concerns, including having been disowned upon coming out.

CHAPTER 17

The Cisgender Partner

When a trans person comes out to their loved one about their
trans identity, it is possible a cisgender partner will feel they
have been betrayed by their partner/spouse. Whether your work is
focused on the individual or the family system, it is critical to work
through this relationship dynamic. If the relationship is to survive this
trust rupture, it is important to give voice to the cisgender partner's
concerns.

Details of the case
Kathryn is a 43-year-old Navajo (Diné) woman. She has been married
to Sylvia (also Navajo; Diné) for 21 years. Together they have three
children between the ages of 12 and 18. Kathryn and Sylvia have been
in counseling for three months. Sylvia came out as a trans woman to
Kathryn before they were married, although she only recently began
expressing her feminine identity. For many years, Sylvia kept her
identity to herself and lived in her daily life as a male (in accordance
with the sex she was assigned at birth).

Exploring clinical material
Two years ago, Sylvia told Kathryn she could not live as a male
anymore. Kathryn, even though she was aware of Sylvia's identity,
felt she had been betrayed by Sylvia. Kathryn was reminded of the
vows she and Sylvia took when they married. The vows said nothing
about her husband becoming her wife.

In working with Sylvia and Kathryn, you are concerned about their communication skills. Kathryn attempts to talk to Sylvia about her concerns, but Sylvia quickly becomes defensive. Consider this:

Kathryn: Last week we talked about ways to be open with one another. I've tried to talk with Sylvia.

Sylvia: [Interrupting] The problem is that you always want to rehash what we've already talked about. How many times do I have to tell you that I'm going to make a medical transition?

Counselor: Sylvia, before we talk about your transition, I wonder if we can slow down and listen to what Kathryn is saying. Kathryn, as you talk about not understanding Sylvia's decision, what are the feelings that you are having?

Kathryn: I feel betrayed by Sylvia. Even though I've known about this since before we were married, I did not think it would ever happen. The children, my co-workers, and our friends are all asking questions, and I just don't know how to deal with all of this. [Kathryn begins to cry.]

Sylvia: What do you mean when you say you feel betrayed? I didn't cheat on you. I don't understand why you don't want me to be happy. [Sylvia's tone is defensive, and her face reddens as her voice gets louder.]

Kathryn: You really don't understand how selfish you are being with this. You haven't talked to the children, and in addition to being confused about what has happened to their father they are experiencing difficulties at school and you can't even see that.

Counselor: Kathryn, let's go back to the idea that you feel betrayed. There is a lot going on, and I will hold these ideas, but when you say you feel betrayed, what does that mean for you?

Kathryn: I love Sylvia, but Sylvia isn't the person I married. I married Larry. How am I supposed to explain this to my co-workers and family? None of them know what "transgender" means.

Sylvia: We talked about my identity many years ago. I thought that

I could live my life as Larry, but the longer I tried to do that, the more I realized I was being dishonest with myself. I know you are hurting, Kathryn, but imagine how much it hurts me to pretend that being a male-identified person is okay. It just isn't, and I can't keep up that facade.

Counselor: It sounds like you are both struggling. I wonder if it's possible for you to see how each other is hurting in the face of your own pain?

The counselor brings up an important idea. Often when a couple comes in for counseling, they have not stopped loving each other, but they are having a hard time listening to one another. Each person is so wrapped up in their own feelings and concerns that they are having a hard time seeing the other person's concerns.

It is common for the trans person in the clinical setting to forget their loved ones have a transition experience of their own. Even though Sylvia and Kathryn have had conversations about Sylvia's identity as many as 21 years ago, Kathryn has not been part of Sylvia's more recent decision to come out and live as a woman. People usually think of betrayal as involving infidelity, but for a trans couple, it can also include the trans person's decision to live in their affirmed identity.

After exploring Kathryn's thoughts about betrayal, the counselor returns to the idea that Kathryn thinks Sylvia is being selfish.

Counselor: Kathryn, earlier you said you thought Sylvia was being selfish by coming out now. What does that mean to you?

Kathryn: Well, for starters [speaking to the counselor], Sylvia expects the children to refer to her as their mother, but I'm their mother. Sylvia was never pregnant, nor did she deliver the children. I did.

Sylvia: Kathryn, I have never assumed that I was the person who gave birth to our children. You are putting words in my mouth [with an angry tone].

Counselor: [To Sylvia and Kathryn] It is really important that you talk to one another in our work together. Sylvia, is it fair to say that you feel misunderstood?

Sylvia: Yes. I guess I can see where Kathryn is coming from, but I think everyone will be safer if the kids refer to me as their mom in public. I worry about how others will respond to their language if it doesn't fit with how I present myself.

Kathryn: [Crying, and stumbling over her words] Sylvia, when do you plan to talk with the children about what this means? You have seen how confused our youngest kids are about what this means for them. They are having a hard enough time understanding what is happening in their own bodies.

Sylvia: I know. What do you want me to say to them [in a conciliatory tone]?

Kathryn: Could we start with making time each week to talk about what this means to you, to them, and the ways this is impacting their lives? You may not be aware of it, but Lucy [their 12-year-old] has been the victim of bullying at school. Other kids are taunting her and calling her names. She comes home from school each day in tears and doesn't want to go to school in the mornings.

Sylvia: I didn't know that was happening.

General commentary

The conversation in the sessions continues to move forward. Even though the basics of the sessions are no different than what you might discuss with a cisgender couple (e.g., good communication skills, slowing down the session to ensure the clients are listening to one another), it is important to understand the nuanced differences that arise when one member of the family system has a trans identity. It is common for the trans person to become overly focused on their own life experiences to the detriment of others in the family system. This focus is not meant to be malicious or mean-spirited. Rather, the trans person is likely managing many aspects of their identity and is unable to hold the challenges that are faced by others in the family system.

As a provider, you are responsible for handling the clinical material in such a way so that each member of the family system feels heard. This may be especially difficult if you have a bias about trans people, regardless of whether this is a positive or negative bias. Both members of this family system deserve to be heard and supported. Helping Sylvia see some of the ways her decision is impacting her wife and their children is important as it will help take some of the pressure off of Kathryn. At the same time, Kathryn can learn the ways to support Sylvia in her planned transition as she learns what Sylvia is facing on a day-to-day basis.

Even though this clinical relationship began as couples counseling, it may be useful to include the children in one or more sessions. This will allow Kathryn and Sylvia to understand the challenges their children are facing.

EXPERT COMMENT

This chapter brings into clear focus a tension that is frequently faced by couples in which one partner is trans and the other is cisgender: between the understandable need for the trans partner to make progress toward living authentically and feeling congruent, and the need to ensure that progress is the product of a "team" approach involving both partners. It is crucial that the trans partner is transparent about the aim of living authentically, the steps that need to be taken to reach that goal, the desired timing of those steps, and the reasons underlying this move (e.g., minority stress). Equally important is that the cisgender partner not only understand the procedures involved with each step but that their emotional response be acknowledged and addressed so they may actively participate in making the decision to move forward.

It is helpful if, at the outset, the goals of the couple's work together are clearly delineated and agreed upon. Often an underlying goal is to remain together as a couple if at all possible. With this goal, a team approach becomes essential, though as this case illustrates, communication and other problems can make this challenging. Quite often, one or both partners may be in individual therapy. If this is the case, it can also be helpful to establish at the outset permission (and appropriate release) as to what information can be shared between the individual and couples therapists.

Even with these steps having been taken carefully at the outset, tension nonetheless exists. It is important to explore with the couple the contributors to the current expression of tension. In the case of Sylvia and Kathryn, communication difficulties are apparent. Other ways to address the needs include an assumption by Sylvia that Kathryn would have continued to expect her to begin a transition at any time and that, because she knew that Sylvia identified as female, this change was inevitable. In this case, Sylvia may need to understand why after several years of not having made any tangible moves toward transition, Kathryn may have thought that such a transition might not occur.

Kathryn's shift is a primary focus for a family that includes young children, rather than simply the two of them. This shift encompasses attention to the needs of their children and how Sylvia's transition may affect their lives, both at home and in other spheres. Kathryn's identity, both as a mother and with regard to her sexual orientation, may also be a concern. Sylvia's transition seems to have triggered questions or doubt for Kathryn about how she identifies.

As these underlying issues are addressed with an improved communication style that ensures that both partners voice their concerns and are heard by the other, the therapist will need to continually calibrate the balance between the needs of the trans partner to live authentically and the goal of ensuring family and couple cohesion. The more the therapist understands each partner's underlying assumptions and needs, the more likely that mutually agreeable goals will be reached.

Expert comment authored by Michael L. Hendricks,
PhD, ABPP, Washington, DC

Take-home messages

The cisgender partner can easily get lost as you work with the trans partner to help them in their transition. Providing space for the cisgender partner may help ensure that the marriage remains intact.

This type of work is much the same as any couples counseling session. You may be working to help the couple develop good communication skills. These skills can be useful not only in the family system, but also in life.

CHAPTER 18

Institutions

R estrooms, prisons and jails, nursing homes, rehabilitation and treatment centers, and in-patient mental health centers are some of the "institutions" that are gender segregated. This means there are usually two, and only two, housing options–male and female. The problem is this configuration does not allow for safe housing for trans individuals. Administrators of these facilities often make a decision without consulting with the client. Further, administrators typically decide to place the trans person according the sex they were assigned at birth. This can be awkward and dangerous for the trans person and the person they are roomed with.

In recent years, there has been an increasing concern from older adults in the LGBTQ+ community. If they need to be housed in nursing or long-term care facilities, they may find they have to go back into the closet (Maddux 2010) because the facility does not welcome LGBTQ+ people. In the following case, I will explore the challenges associated with in-patient treatment.

Details of the case

Kale is a 38-year-old Hawai'ian who was assigned female at birth. Kale has a non-binary identity and uses the pronouns they/them/their. Kale had their first psychotic break at the age of 23. They have been in and out of mental health facilities for the past 15 years. Several years ago, Kale stopped taking their medication, and after they broke into a store, the police responded and took Kale into custody. We see on the following pages how Kale's case plays out.

Exploring clinical material

Kale first came to your attention when they were referred to the in-patient mental health facility in which you worked. At the time, Kale identified as a female and therefore they were admitted for treatment in your women's facility. Kale had an androgynous presentation. They were fairly boisterous and tended to be disruptive in group activities. Since your program was built around group activities, this made their treatment and that of the other clients difficult. You worked individually with Kale and tried to help them stay focused in group activities, but the best results were that Kale might be able to fully participate in one group meeting a day.

Several years later you are working for a private in-patient facility. Once again, Kale stopped taking their medication, which led to a psychotic break. Kale's insurance has approved treatment to achieve and maintain stability. On intake, Kale mentions to the intake worker that they have a non-binary identity and do not feel safe sharing a room with either a man or a woman. They go on to say they do not feel safe with a man and they do not want to cause discomfort to a woman. You meet with Kale the next day and get reacquainted. Kale tells you that they have been feeling really good and even have a part-time job. They are still living with family members and for the most part that is going well. When asked what led to them stopping their medications, Kale responds that they were having trouble with their finances and could not afford their medication. Most of the medications are relatively inexpensive, but one of the drugs has increased in price to the point that Kale could no longer afford to purchase the drug.

The psychiatrist, who refuses to use gender-neutral pronouns, assesses Kale and their need for medications. This provider changes Kale's medications. While at the in-patient facility, Kale has no idea what these medications will cost. Kale is also very tired of seeing the psychiatrist since he refuses to use gender-neutral pronouns and even attempts to have Kale moved to a room with a male client. You have worked with this psychiatrist for a few years and are aware he does not use an affirmative practice as it relates to trans people. Even though you have tried to correct his use of pronouns in staffing meetings, you know he is unlikely to change. You have tried to bring this problem to management, but your complaint has largely been ignored.

Kale: I am not going to work with that psychiatrist again. I am so tired of him ignoring my pronouns. It feels like he is purposefully screwing it up.

Counselor: Dr. Jeffries? [Kale nods.] I wish we had more psychiatric providers. He has been working here for about 20 years and it is hard to get him to change his ways.

Kale: How do you let him get away with that? I feel like I take three or four steps backward after meeting with him because he doesn't respect me.

Counselor: I have noticed that. It is one of the reasons why I make sure to meet with you after you have seen him.

Kale: In some ways, it feels like you are part of the problem then— since you know he is just going to hurt me.

Counselor: I can see how it would feel that way. It is as if I am standing by letting him treat you poorly.

Kale: Exactly. I would like to get out of this place, but as long as he is part of my treatment plan, I do not see how that would be possible.

This case highlights many of the concerns that trans people face in medical facilities. From housing concerns to affirmative language, there are many ways that a trans person's identity can be erased or ignored. This has consequences for the trans person and their own sense of well-being.

EXPERT COMMENT

As a provider working within an established gender clinic in a metropolitan area in the Midwest, surrounded by more rural areas with limited gender services, working with trans and non-binary clients in institutional settings is a frequent occurrence.

Working with clients in institutional settings calls on the mental healthcare provider to lean in to their role as an advocate and to take a systems perspective. The clinical example in this chapter illustrates several key points that are important for providers to address. First is the intersectional experience of the client within the system. Kale is not only navigating concerns around their gender identity in a non-affirming environment, but also economic and class concerns as well as stigma of mental illness that limit the client's agency in their own treatment and care. As mental healthcare providers, it is our responsibility to have a critical consciousness and awareness of how these intersecting systemic oppressions impact our clients and to advocate as best we can within these systems for the client's best care. This might mean taking a more active approach in finding gender-affirming psychiatric care, or lobbying within the institution for policies that enforce gender-affirming practices, including utilizing legislation and professional association policies to pressure institutions to shift their policies and practices. A common concern is housing, and mental healthcare providers can advocate for clients by calling ahead and asking about housing policies, providing information on gender-affirming policies, and problem solving with in-patient providers to create a more gender-affirming environment for their clients.

Additionally, mental healthcare providers must take a systems perspective, rather than the more typical psychotherapy focus on individuals. Someone who is living in a group home, or is incarcerated, may have concerns that will not be encapsulated within just their individual experience. Multiple systems are impacting their well-being and their gendered experiences. Clinically, this may mean bringing ancillary connections within the client's life into the session. For example, a client living within a group home who wishes to socially transition and begin hormone therapy, and who also has a medical guardian, would benefit from having group home staff attend partial sessions to engage the staff in supporting gender-affirming interactions for the clients. Group home staff and guardians can be included in medical appointments as well as therapy sessions in order to develop gender-affirming treatment plans and can serve to provide psychoeducation for all about how to implement gender-affirming changes. Another example may be working as an advocate for trans and non-binary clients who are incarcerated in providing gender-affirming training or materials and offering joint sessions in order to increase understanding and affirmation within the client's experience. Since policies vary from state to state about access to gender-affirming interventions, collaborating with LGBTQ+ advocacy groups can also be helpful in advocating for clients and improving their well-being.

In summary, in working with trans and non-binary clients within institutional settings, mental healthcare providers are called upon to take a systems perspective, step into advocacy roles, provide psychoeducation, and consider the impact of intersecting systemic oppression on our clients' lives in order to provide gender-competent affirming care.

Expert comment authored by Katie Spencer, PhD, Minneapolis, MN

Take-home messages

Although this chapter focuses on the issues associated with housing trans people in a medical facility, even more danger can arise for a trans person who is incarcerated. Jails and prisons are sex segregated. Prison and jail administrators most often will place a trans person in a facility based on one of the following: (a) sex assigned at birth, (b) presence of male/female genitalia, or (c) impression of a person's gender identity. Baus, Hunt, and Williams (2006) directed a documentary that follows the lives of trans women who have been incarcerated. Story after story recounts the abuse that trans feminine people experienced in prisons and jails. Trans prisoners are physically, sexually, and emotionally abused and assaulted in prisons. It is not uncommon that guards will look the other way or participate in the abuse.

One of the ways trans people might be housed is in solitary confinement (also known as segregation). According to the eighth amendment of the U.S. Constitution, "excessive bail shall not be required, nor excessive fines imposed, nor cruel and unusual punishments inflicted" (U.S. Const. amend. VIII). Placing a person into segregation "for their own protection" constitutes cruel and unusual punishment. A trans person should be housed according to the sentence based on the crime committed. Placing a person in segregation may go beyond the intended sentence. Further, placing a person in solitary confinement has the potential to create significant mental health issues for the person being confined (*Davenport v. DeRobertis* 1988).

Another issue, and one of the reasons why trans people are sometimes placed in solitary confinement, is that they become the target of rape and other types of sexual assault. In 2003 the Prison Rape Elimination Act (PREA) was passed with unanimous support from all members of the U.S. Congress. PREA provided "for the analysis of the incidence and effects of prison rape in federal, state, and local institutions and to provide information, resources, recommendations and funding to protect individuals from prison rape" (Prison Rape Elimination Act 2003, §30303(a)(1)). In 2005, the first year in which data was collected, it was estimated that over 6000 people experienced sexual victimization (Bureau of Justice Statistics 2018). By 2018, that number had risen to nearly 25,000. The guidelines for PREA were revised in 2012 (National PREA Resource Center 2020). The 2012 guidelines required that facilities provide multiple ways for inmates to report rape and that the facility investigate each allegation. Records from this new law include the total number of allegations, how many were substantiated, the number under investigation, the number unfounded (i.e., did not happen), and the number that were unsubstantiated (i.e., there was not enough evidence to prove the claim) (Santo 2018). Over the time that the PREA has been in place, between 6 and 10 percent of incidents were found to have happened. Between 2012 and 2015, about 8.5 percent of allegations were deemed to be true (Santo 2018). Although the Bureau of Justice Statistics estimates that 200,000 inmates are sexually assaulted in prisons and jails in the U.S. on an annual basis, the reports do not come close to that number and the vast majority of reports are not substantiated.

The final consideration for trans people who are incarcerated is the ability to access medical treatment while in prison. It is likely easier to secure hormones in prison than it is to obtain gender reassignment surgery (GRS). Levine (2016) reports that requests for GRS tend to come from people who have long-term or life sentences. Levine goes on to compare the treatment for prostate cancer (which may be curable through treatment) to gender dysphoria and the various treatment options (e.g., GRS, tracheal shave, augmentation mammoplasty) that serve to "cure" the trans person of their gender dysphoria. It is critical for people who are incarcerated that there be an available diagnosis to address gender dysphoria and its stated medical necessity. If treatment is not medically necessary, it is unlikely an incarcerated trans person will be able to access treatment. Some trans people who have been detained have difficulty accessing care (White Hughto and Clark 2019). Challenges include mistreatment by healthcare providers or denial of care, which can have significant implications including suicide attempts and completions (Glezer, McNiel, and Binder 2013). Trans people, whether or not they have been found guilty of a criminal offense, deserve healthcare regardless of the clinical concern. Gender dysphoria is a valid clinical concern that has numerous effective treatments, most of which are medically necessary.

CHAPTER 19

Advocating for Medical Needs

One of the most common complaints from trans people about medical care is the need to educate their provider (Grant et al. 2011; James et al. 2016). This happens in all areas of care (i.e., medical, psychiatric, psychological). On average, in undergraduate medical training, students receive 60 minutes of training on LGBTQ+ people (Obedin-Maliver et al. 2011). This is hardly enough time to even introduce basic knowledge about LGBTQ+ people. Obviously when an LGBTQ+ person has bladder cancer there is no difference in how the condition would be treated as compared to a cisgender person. However, when their partner or spouse shows up to visit them in the hospital, they should not be greeted with 20 questions about who they are and be required to repeatedly show documentation of their relationship.

When a trans person is seeking trans-specific healthcare, their provider should have the competence to care for their client with dignity and respect. This means trans people should **never**:

- receive sexual advances
- be ridiculed
- be denied care
- suffer staff use of the wrong name or pronouns.

Although these seem like sensible expectations, I have experienced all of these as recently as the fall of 2018. Trans people should be able to walk into a medical provider's office without fear for their physical or emotional safety. Far too often trans people postpone care because they fear the ways in which they will be treated by a provider or their staff (James et al. 2016). In this chapter I explore the ways trans people can advocate for their own needs in healthcare settings.

Details of the case

Blake is a 55-year-old African American person with a non-binary identity who was assigned female at birth. Prior to transition 25 years ago, Blake identified as a lesbian. Today Blake is in a polyamorous relationship. Blake's partners, Calli and Dave, are aware of Blake's gender identity. Blake does not use pronouns as even though people have started using non-binary pronouns such as they/them/their, Blake does not feel any connection to pronouns.

Exploring clinical material

Recently, Blake has been experiencing severe abdominal cramping. Blake has not been to a doctor since 2015. Blake has generally avoided the doctor because of difficult and embarrassing experiences. Blake tried to stay current with health recommendations but has tired of explaining to medical providers about the healthcare needs that should be addressed. Blake has a family history of ovarian cancer and is worried the cramping is related to this.

Blake has generally been in good health. Blake looks for a provider covered by Blake's health insurance plan. Blake picks the provider that is closest to work as this will make it easier to get to appointments. The doctor's office sends Blake some paperwork to complete prior to the first appointment. As Blake works through the paperwork Blake thinks this might be the wrong provider. The paperwork seems very oriented to cisgender and heteronormative experiences.

When Blake arrives at the first appointment, the front desk worker insists Blake use pronouns. Blake tries to explain there are no pronouns that fit. The front desk worker begins to raise his voice and Blake just wants to turn around and run out of the office. Other clients have stopped what they were doing and now are focused on the commotion at the front desk. Blake says, "There is no reason why this should be that important. I simply need to find out what is wrong with me." Another employee steps in and asks what the issue is. This person accepts Blake's paperwork as it was presented.

Understandably, Blake is uncertain about how the rest of the appointment experience will unfold. Blake knows there is something wrong and it is important to get it checked out. At this point, Blake wishes that one of Blake's partners had been able to come to the appointment. Within a few minutes Blake is called back. The medical assistant takes all of the usual information (e.g., height, weight, blood pressure, pulse). The medical assistant asks about the reason for the visit. Blake talks about having abdominal pain that has become increasingly difficult to ignore. Blake then mentions the family history of ovarian cancer. The medical assistant looks confused. Blake then provides information about being a transgender person and having been assigned female at birth. The medical assistant still does not understand. This leads to yet another difficult interaction with the staff in this medical office. Blake is wondering if it is worth it.

The medical assistant leaves the examination room. Blake decides this is the best time to leave the office. Blake walks out the door and departs. When Blake gets home, Calli asks how the appointment went. Blake recounts the story and says no examination happened and the pain really is not that bad anymore. Calli can see this is not true but decides not to make a big issue out of it at this time.

Six months later, Blake is still having cramping, and now there is an abdominal mass and the pain is constant. Blake's partners have been begging Blake to go to the doctor and both have stated they will accompany Blake to the appointment. Blake's experience at the next provider is even worse than the first. The new provider was recommended by a friend of Blake's. Dave and Calli go to the appointment but are very disappointed. Even though this provider seems to understand the needs of transgender people, Blake is dismissed by the provider and told to get care elsewhere.

The obstacles Blake faced are examples of just a few of the concerns trans people have when they attempt to address their healthcare needs. Blake's situation highlights some of the reasons why trans people postpone care to the point there is nothing a provider can do because the individual has waited too long (Byne et al. 2018).

Counselor: Hi Blake. Where would you like to begin today?

Blake: I do not know if I will ever be able to find a provider who understands my health concerns and is willing to treat me.

Counselor: That's right, you had an appointment about your abdominal pain last week. Did Dave and Calli go with you?

Blake: They did. But that did not help one bit. The doctor barely conducted an exam and as I explained my identity and who Dave and Calli were to me, he told me to leave the office.

Counselor: Oh dear, that certainly isn't how we hoped that would go.

Blake: No, it wasn't. I just feel completely defeated right now. I know there is something wrong with me, but I just cannot find a provider in town who seems willing to see me.

Counselor: This is the third provider right?

Blake: No, the second. I didn't follow up after the last one–I didn't want to admit that I was hurting as much as I was–partly because I knew this would happen again.

Counselor: I would like to talk about how you are finding providers, but right now, I just want to know what you need from me by way of support.

Names, pronouns, and demographic data

Most intake forms used by healthcare providers will have one or more places to indicate information about the client's basic demographic data. These intake forms are relatively simple for cisgender people as the provider is asking questions that fit with the person's identity. Trans people are typically forced to out themselves when completing paperwork. Some transgender people have not changed their name in all aspects of their life. This may include using the name they were assigned at birth on employment records and identification such as a driver's license. One of the first requirements of a new patient is to provide their driver's license and insurance card. When the name on these documents does not match the person's identity, the response can be demoralizing.

If a provider insists on check boxes for information such as gender and marital status, it is critical that a wide variety of options be available. Imagine if Blake was completing an intake form and under gender the choices were male and female and in the marital status section the choices were single, married, divorced, and widowed. Blake would not have a place to list either gender or marital status in a way consistent with Blake's lived experience.

When the medical assistant takes the patient to the exam room it is important to ask the patient what pronouns they use. Invariably, if a person's pronouns are anything other than she/her/hers or he/him/his, the provider and their staff will make a mistake. It is imperative that the provider admit their mistake, as this will help the patient feel the provider is making an effort and that the patient does not have to make the correction. Equally important with regard to pronouns is to avoid using the phrase *preferred pronoun*. Although you might hear a trans person use this language, most do not *prefer* the use of a particular pronoun, or none at all. Rather, they insist upon it as an indication they are being treated with dignity and respect.

Treating the organ systems that are present

One of the challenges trans people face is confusion about the types of care a person needs. This confusion can be with either the provider or the patient. In short, providers should treat the organ systems that are present. In the case of Blake, it is possible the diagnosis will be ovarian cancer. If Blake's providers read Blake as being male, they will wonder why Blake provided information about the last menstrual cycle and other questions typically associated with health for females. Also, if Blake is read as male, providers may be concerned about prostate issues and may even try to convince Blake there is a need for a prostate exam.

It may seem like common sense to expect medical providers to treat the organ systems that are present; however, providers assuming the presence or absence of health concerns based on the perception of gender is problematic, as the assumption is far too often wrong for trans patients. The result can be a failure to make a diagnosis of a life-threatening condition.

Mental health provider's role

The role of the mental health provider is both to help their client to process these difficult experiences in the healthcare setting and to provide letters of support as needed (see Appendix B). Helping the client process the experiences they endure in the healthcare setting may require the mental health professional to examine their own biases and assumptions. Even if a person has worked with trans people for some period of time, there are likely still some areas for growth and exploration.

Providing support may take on different roles based on the needs of your client. It may be helpful for the client to practice how they will interact with another person in a healthcare setting. Using real play activities can allow the client the opportunity to respond to different scenarios so they are less reactive in the moment. This does not mean they should not be offended, rather they can be present in the moment and ask for what they need. Being able to advocate for one's self is an important skill that may need to be learned. Not everyone is able to ask for what they need especially if they have the sense they are not understood by the other party. These are some of the issues a person might need to advocate for:

- the kind and amount of medication they take

- whether or not they have a private room in a hospital

- the frequency with which they access treatment

- the need for referral to a different provider

- the right to access their health record

- the right to make decisions about their healthcare, including who else would have that right.

Too often people do not speak up when they have questions or when they think a different approach is needed for their care. Yes, doctors are smart and would not be doctors if that were not the case. However, given all of the options, the client is the one who gets to make the final choice about their care.

EXPERT COMMENT

Creating a clinical setting that demonstrates dignity and respect for all patients, regardless of sexual orientation, gender identity, and gender expression, is central to patient-centered care. It is also in line with priorities to reduce health disparities among LGBTQ+ people (Institute of Medicine 2011). To reduce barriers to care and increase the likelihood of appropriate healthcare utilization and health optimization among this vulnerable and at-risk patient group, the following recommendations are made.

Gender-affirming care is patient-centered care

Awareness of patient demographics, cultural characteristics, lifestyle factors, and related social determinants of health offers clinicians important data to inform an accurate history and physical examination and may help in risk stratification, diagnostic differentials, and the delivery of effective treatment plans. Clinicians achieve optimal health outcomes through the use of communication strategies that focus on individual patient needs and preferences. *How* and *what* we communicate to patients (verbal, nonverbal, and visual) conveys our level of care and concern. In addition to inclusive and gender-affirming intake forms to accurately assess transgender and non-binary patients' demographics and medical history, we recommend routine implementation of the following techniques to increase transgender and non-binary patients' comfort and engagement in their medical care.

Set the stage and agenda. Introduce yourself using language that demonstrates gender-affirming practices (e.g., "My name is...and I go by..."; "My pronouns are..."). Introduce your role in promoting health, and if relevant, your role within your team. Inform patients of the routine nature of all questions and review conditions of confidentiality. Ask for patients' pronouns ("What pronouns would you like me to use?") and name ("What name would you like me to use during our visits?"). Solicit patients' presenting concern(s) and goal(s) for visit.

Ask open-ended questions. Frame questions in a manner that generates increased patient information (e.g., "What are you most worried about?" or "What do you think is contributing to your pain?"). Closed-ended questions should be used sparingly.

Use gender-neutral language. Initially use gender-neutral terms to describe sensitive areas of the body, which may otherwise elicit feelings of dysphoria/distress (e.g., "chest" vs. "breast"; "external genitalia" vs. "vulva"). Subsequently, use the same terms used by the patient during the visit.

Be inclusive and gender-affirming in the sexual history. Normalize routine sexual history taking by providing the rationale behind questions. Reinforce confidentiality. Ask sexual history questions such as:

Have you *ever* been sexually active?

What is/are the sex *and* gender of your partner(s)?

How many sexual partners have you had in the last *12 months*?

What types of sexual activity do you have?

When was the last time you got tested for STIs?

Respond using nonjudgmental and affirming language (e.g., "partner" vs. "wife/husband"; "internal condom" vs. "female condom").

Minimize distress related to physical exams and sensitive procedures. When taking an organ history, explain your rationale for asking and how the information informs your clinical reasoning and management plans. Recognize that transgender and non-binary individuals may use materials/devices that reduce gender dysphoria by modifying their visible gender characteristics (e.g., chest binders to reduce the appearance of breasts, body contouring pads to modify body shape). Be prepared to acknowledge these materials/devices (e.g., "I noticed you're wearing a binder, can you tell me more about it?") and provide the patient with privacy, as appropriate. Discuss if materials/devices are causing physical symptoms or discomfort.

- Ask for permission before asking sensitive questions or performing any sensitive examinations or procedures; explain rationale and techniques prior to examination; offer patients the option of having a medical chaperone, if available, during a sensitive exam.

- Become familiar with alternative means of obtaining specimens (e.g., self-swab vs. clinician collected).

- Do not provide commentary on aesthetics of gender-affirming surgeries (e.g., do not state "Your vagina looks real" or "I would not have been able to tell that you previously had a penis").

Shared decision-making. Present evidence-based treatment recommendations and solicit patients' reactions and buy-in. Co-create a treatment plan acceptable to the patient. Use the SHARE Approach[7] to engage the patient in their healthcare decision making (Agency for Healthcare Research and Quality 2016).

Acknowledge mistakes and knowledge gaps. Apologize for miscommunications or mistakes if they occur; acknowledge deficits in knowledge of specific transgender and non-binary patient concerns, as needed; reaffirm your commitment to providing the highest quality of care to *all* of your patients; and engage in self-directed learning to address knowledge gaps to increase engagement of LGBTQ+ patients. To increase the understanding of the experiences of transgender and non-binary patients, we recommend building familiarity with the following concepts:

- **Broken arm syndrome**: Describes the tendency for clinicians to attribute or relate any medical concern to a patient's gender identity or expression. This phenomenon is likely a result of cognitive biases (e.g., availability heuristic, anchoring heuristic, premature closure). When used, it undermines comprehensive medical evaluation and invalidates patients' experiences.

- **Minority stress**: Describes the unique social stressors experienced by LGBTQ+ patients owing to their minority identity status(es) (e.g., prejudice, stigma, discrimination, violence). These experiences may further undermine health and well-being (Hendricks and Testa 2012).

- **Medical mistrust**: Describes a feeling of uneasiness or worry experienced by many transgender and gender diverse patients in relation to healthcare engagement and may result in care avoidance. Origins of medical mistrust include individual and collective experiences of medical exploitation, mistreatment, and invalidation. Assume that you will need to actively and intentionally build trust with your transgender and gender diverse patient population.

- **Trauma-informed care**: A framework that proactively acknowledges and responds to the consequences of trauma on the biological, psychological, and psychological components of a person's life (Chang et al. 2018).

Clinicians have an obligation to practice within their competency and ensure that patient health needs are adequately addressed (American Psychological Association 2017). Although perhaps less familiar, transgender and non-binary identity characteristics alone are *not* beyond the *clinical scope* of any clinician. When limits to expertise arise, clinicians should offer specific and appropriate referrals to transgender and non-binary patients in order to limit barriers to care and promote longitudinal engagement with health services. To make appropriate referrals, we recommend the following:

- Establish a referral list that identifies local clinicians who specialize in LGBTQ+ healthcare. When possible, establish ongoing relationships with these clinicians to increase ease of referral.

- Contact national organizations and/or medical institutions who promote LGBTQ+ healthcare for additional guidance, resources, and recommendations.

Expert comment authored by Tyson L. Pankey, PhD, MPH, and Cesar A. Gonzalez, PhD, LP, ABPP, both of Rochester, MN

Take-home messages

The primary take-home message from this chapter is the importance of treating trans patients with dignity and respect. Additionally, it is imperative that clinicians allow a trans person the space to have a voice about how to address their treatment needs. People are rarely taught to advocate for themselves. They tend to believe the provider must know all of the answers for the health concern(s) they are facing. Although there may be some truth to this, this does not mean that a person cannot ask for different treatment options.

It is hard to ask for help. Asking for help in a culturally appropriate manner becomes that much more difficult when a person does not feel well. It is not enough for a provider to ask if the patient (client) has any questions. Providers must anticipate the types of questions a person might have and be ready to have those discussions. Encourage your clients to ask for a longer appointment if they have multiple concerns that need to be addressed. Most people never consider that. Clients can advocate for their needs, and although this is challenging, it will hopefully lead to being able to receive necessary care.

CHAPTER 20

Summary and Conclusion

In this book, I have attempted to create a resource unlike any other for mental health providers. This book addresses clinical concerns that may arise for your clients and patients when they have a trans identity. This certainly is not an exhaustive case book. I hope, though, that one of the things you will see is that working with the clinical issues that your trans clients bring to the session may closely resemble the issues your cisgender clients want to talk about. They may want to talk about job dissatisfaction, communication issues in their relationship, fertility concerns, or bullying. What makes these issues different for trans and non-binary people is that more often than not there are few if any protections against discrimination and other forms of mistreatment. This adds a layer of complexity to your work as you may need to hold the anger and frustration that your client is experiencing relative to systemic oppression.

It is common to make mistakes when referring to your client. Make a simple, brief apology and carry on. It is unacceptable to start using a client's dead name or the pronouns that are consistent with the sex they were assigned at birth when you learn of their trans history. It is also unacceptable to ask a trans or non-binary person about their genitals unless you have a legitimate reason to do so. If you want to know if a client is planning a medical transition that may include genital surgery, simply ask them what their goals for transition are. This avoids the awkward conversation about a person's genitals. If it is not acceptable for a trans person to ask a cisgender person about their genitals, then trans people should be offered the same level of respect and privacy.

It is my sincere hope that the information in this book will be a resource for many years to come. When I transitioned in 1999, I knew that part of my journey would be to help make the world safe for trans and non-binary people. Like me, trans and non-binary people often walk into new situations with a bit of fear and trepidation. This is more than simply being in a new situation. It is also a legitimate worry about whether they can be honest about who they are and what they need.

Endnotes

1   Cross-sex behavior is in quotes in the text as there really is no such thing. It is an artificial demarcation to state some toys or clothes are only for boys or only for girls. Gender is a social construction. Gender is also on a spectrum. As such, there is no such thing as cross-sex behavior.

2   GnRH treatment, or puberty blockers, is a treatment method that is used to delay (eliminate) puberty for adolescents. This is commonly started at Tanner Stage 2 or the initiation of puberty. It effectively blocks the effects of an endogenous puberty and allows the adolescent more time in deciding about their trans identity without experiencing puberty.

3   GSAs (which were originally called Gay–Straight alliances) began in the 1980s. They are also known as Queer–Straight Alliances. Kevin Jennings is credited with starting the first GSA. He went on to found GLSEN (originally known as the Gay, Lesbian, and Straight Educators Network).

4   Dead naming is the practice of using the name a person was given rather than the name that is affirmed. For the trans person, this is disrespectful.

5   Queer is a term that was first used as an epithet toward gay men and lesbians. Members of the LGBTQ+ community, especially those under the age of 30, have reclaimed this term and it is used as an identity term. It can mean that a person does not identify on the gender binary, and as such gay or lesbian does not fit their experience.

6   In this sentence "their" is used as a non-binary pronoun.

7   The SHARE Approach includes the following steps: (a) **S**eek your patient's participation, (b) **H**elp your patient explore and compare treatment models, (c) **A**ssess your patient's values and preferences, (d) **R**each a decision with your patient, and (e) **E**valuate your patient's decision (Agency for Healthcare Research and Quality 2016).

Trans Conferences and Other Organizations

- Gender Odyssey Conference
- Gender Spectrum
- GLSEN
- Jim Collins Foundation
- Lambda Legal
- My Bandana Project
- National Center for Transgender Equality
- Philadelphia Trans Wellness Conference
- Sylvia Rivera Law Project
- The Transgender Law and Policy Institute
- The Trevor Project
- Trans Lifeline
- Trans Student Educational Resources
- TransYouth Family Allies
- Transgender Law Center
- Transgender Legal Defense & Education Fund
- World Professional Association for Transgender Health

Sample Letters of Referral

Trans and non-binary people need letters of referral for several reasons. If your patient wants to make a medical transition, they may need a letter of referral either to initiate hormone treatment or for surgery. Your clients may also need a letter when they are seeking a name change or gender marker changes, or to school administrators. Although there are no real guidelines for letters that are written to address social and legal concerns, the examples provided here should help address the needs of your clients. On the following pages you will find a letter for (a) hormone treatment, (b) surgical care, (c) a name or gender marker change, and (d) classroom accommodation.

Dear Medical Provider,

I am writing to introduce you to my client {client's name: James} (DOB: 01/01/2000; client's legal name is Jennifer Smith). I am a licensed psychologist in the State of Arizona (License No.: PSY-01234). My client uses the pronouns he/him/his.

I have been working with James for nine months. James first identified as trans at the age of 12. James's identity has been consistent, and he is out to family, friends, and co-workers. James would like to initiate testosterone treatment. We have talked at length about what testosterone will or will not accomplish. James has a good understanding of this and is able to give informed consent.

James has a history of depression and this is well-controlled with counseling and medication. James attempted suicide when he was a teenager. This was directly related to a lack of support from his father and difficulties he was experiencing in school. He states that he has not ever felt that way since then.

James is in a two-year relationship and they have two children. James works as a computer technician and states that he enjoys his work.

James meets the diagnostic criteria for gender dysphoria (F64.1) [Note: I do not always include this, and when I do, I talk with my client about what it means to have that included]. In my professional opinion, James is ready to begin testosterone treatment. I am available to answer any questions and will continue to work with James as he begins hormone treatment. I can be reached at (888) 555-1212.

Sincerely,
lore m. dickey, PhD, LP

Dear Surgeon,

I am referring Jayden Wright {client's name; you may need to include the legal name} to you for chest masculinization surgery. I have been working with Jayden for three months. He was referred to me by his previous provider as she did not have experience with trans masculine clients.

Jayden is currently working as an accountant at a firm that manages tax returns. Jayden has been in this line of work for eight years. He finds the work very enjoyable and understands how he will need to adjust his work as he recovers from surgery.

Jayden is single but reports that he has several friends who will help him with meals, rides for follow-up care, and household chores. These friends have a good understanding of what Jayden will experience as they are also trans. Jayden's mental health history is unremarkable. He has good coping skills including a daily meditation practice. I have no concerns about Jayden's readiness.

I am available to consult should the need arise. Jayden is aware of the challenges associated with the surgery and has engaged in an informed consent process. I can be reached at (888) 555-1212 should you need to reach me.

Sincerely,
lore m. dickey, PhD, LP

Note: This letter will change if the client is seeking genital surgery. There might be a need to include information about understanding changes to fertility. It is also important to note that a client may need two letters for genital surgery from referees, one of whom has doctoral level training.

Dear XXXXXX,

I am writing a letter to introduce BeverLee Addison. BeverLee is a trans woman, and she would like to change her name {or gender marker}. BeverLee has identified as female for 18 months and would like for her identification to be consistent with her identity. BeverLee has been working with me and I agree that it is time for her identity documents to be consistent.

Should there be questions about this request, I can be reached at (888) 555-1212. Thank you for your attention to this matter.

Sincerely,
lore m. dickey, PhD, LP

Note: In this letter, there is little attention to the client's mental health. This may need to be adjusted depending on the requirements of the jurisdiction where the name or gender marker changes are being made. It is important to understand the laws and regulations in the area where you see patients.

Dear Course Instructor,

I am writing on behalf of Justice Maxwell. Justice is enrolled in a course with you this academic term. Justice, whose legal name is {legal name here}, goes by the name Justice and uses gender-neutral pronouns (e.g., they/them/their).

Although you will find Justice's legal name on your course roster, we ask that you use their affirmed name and pronouns.

Should you have any questions, I can be reached at (888) 555-1212.

Sincerely,
lore m. dickey, PhD, LP

Note: This is really about addressing the power distance between the student and their course instructor. Students use nicknames all the time. There is no reason why a trans or non-binary student should not be able to as well.

Resources for Active Duty, Reserve, and Veteran Service Members

Tips for working with transgender service members and veterans

- Make space for gender diversity in your practice with service members and veterans:

  - Familiarize yourself with Department of Defense and Department of Veterans Affairs policies and resources related to gender identity.

    » DTM 19-004

      www.esd.whs.mil/Portals/54/Documents/
      DD/issuances/dtm/DTM%2019-004.
      PDF?ver=2020-03-17-140438-090

      www.palmcenter.org/wp-content/uploads/2019/04/
      The-Making-of-a-Ban.pdf

    » VA Policy

      https://www.patientcare.va.gov/LGBT/index.asp

- – Review professional standards of care and guidelines related to transgender care.

  - » World Professional Association for Transgender Health (WPATH)

    www.wpath.org

  - » American Psychological Association Guidelines

    www.apa.org/practice/guidelines/transgender.pdf

- – Connect with trans-affirming providers in your local community.

- – Take advantage of professional development opportunities to learn more about gender-affirming care and seek consultation as needed.

- Make space for service members and veterans in your gender-affirming practice:

  - – Consider the impact of military policy and experiences on therapeutic alliance and informed consent.

  - – Include questions about military service in your intake paperwork and ask about military history and military-related trauma exposure during the clinical interview.

  - – Support the patient's autonomy in making decisions about their military career and transition process.

  - – Collaborate with VA providers as needed and connect with your local LGBTQ+ Veteran Care Coordinator.

  - – Take advantage of professional development opportunities to learn more about caring for service members and veterans and seek consultation as needed.

Transgender military support and advocacy resources

- SPART*A
  - https://spartapride.org
- Transgender American Veterans Association
  - http://transveteran.org
- Modern Military Association of America
  - https://modernmilitary.org
- Minority Veterans of America
  - www.minorityvets.org
- Local Veterans Affairs LGBTQ+ Veteran Care Coordinator
  - www.patientcare.va.gov/LGBTQ+/index.asp

Don't forget your state and local LGBTQ+ community centers and organizations!

Medical Resources

- Gay and Lesbian Medical Association
  - www.GLMA.org
- Human Rights Campaign
  - www.hrc.org/resources/transgender-patient-services-support-resources-for-providers-and-hospital-a
- National LGBTQ+ Cancer Network
  - https://cancer-network.org
- National LGBTQIA+ Health Education Center
  - www.lgbthealtheducation.org
- The SHARE Approach
  - www.ahrq.gov/health-literacy/curriculum-tools/shared-decisionmaking
- World Professional Association for Transgender Health
  - www.wpath.org

References

Achenbach, T. (2001) *Child Behavior Checklist for Ages 6–18.* Burlington, VT: Achenbach System of Empirically Based Assessment.

Agency for Healthcare Research and Quality (2016) *The SHARE Approach: A Model for Shared Decision Making.* Accessed on 05/14/2020 at www.ahrq. gov/sites/default/files/publications/files/share-approach_factsheet.pdf

American Psychiatric Association (2000) *Diagnostic and Statistical Manual of Mental Disorders* (IV-TR). Alexandria, VA: Author.

American Psychiatric Association (2013) *Diagnostic and Statistical Manual of Mental Disorders* (5th ed.). Washington, DC: Author.

American Psychological Association (2015) 'Guidelines for Psychological Practice with Transgender and Gender Nonconforming People.' *American Psychologist, 70*(9), 832–864. http://dx.doi.org/10.1037/a0039906

American Psychological Association (2017) 'Ethical Principles of Psychologists and Code of Conduct.' Accessed on 05/25/2020 at www. apa.org/ethics/code

American Psychological Association of Graduate Students Committee on Sexual Orientation and Gender Diversity (2018) 'APAGS Climate Guide for LGBTQ+ and Allied Students and Professionals (2nd ed.).' Accessed on 05/17/2020 at www.apa.org/apags/resources/clgbt-climate-guide.pdf

Aragon, S. R., Poteat, V. P., Espelage, D. L., and Koenig B. W. (2014) 'The Influence of Peer Victimization on Educational Outcomes for LGBTQ and Non-LGBTQ High School Students.' *Journal of LGBTQ+ Youth, 11*(1), 1–19. http://dx.doi.org/10.1080/19361653.2014.840761

Ashley, F. and Baril, A. (2018) 'Why "Rapid-Onset Gender Dysphoria" Is Bad Science.' *The Conversation.* Accessed on 05/13/2020 at https:// theconversation.com/why-rapid-onset-gender-dysphoria-is-bad-science-92742

Barr, S. M., Budge, S. L., and Adelson, J. L. (2016) 'Transgender Community Belongingness as a Mediator Between Strength of Transgender Identity and Well-Being.' *Journal of Counseling Psychology, 63*(1), 87–97. http:// dx.doi.org/10.1037/cou0000127

Baus, J., Hunt, D., and Williams, R. (Directors) (2006) *Cruel and Unusual: Transgender Women in Prison* [Film]. Los Angeles: Reid Productions. Accessed on 05/13/2020 at www.youtube.com/watch?v=5Yzy8oh5Fw0

Benjamin, H. (1966) *The Transsexual Phenomenon: All the Facts About the Changing of Sex Through Hormones and Surgery.* New York, NY: Warner Books.

Blosnich, J. R., Marsiglio, M. C., Ditcher, M. E., Gao, S. et al. (2017) 'Impact of Social Determinants of Health on Medical Conditions Among Transgender Veterans.' *American Journal of Preventative Medicine, 52*(4), 491–498. https://doi.org/10.1016/j.amepre.2016.12.019

Bureau of Justice Statistics (2018) *Sexual Victimization Reported by Adult Correctional Authorities, 2012–15.* Accessed on 05/13/2020 at www.bjs. gov/index.cfm?ty=pbdetail&iid=6326

Burnes, T. (2017) 'Flying Faster than the Birds and the Bees: Toward a Sex-Positive Theory and Practice in Multicultural Education.' In R. K. Gordon, T. Akutsu, C. J. McDermott, and J. W. Lalas (eds) *Challenges Associated with Cross-Cultural and At-Risk Student Engagement* (pp.170–187). Hershey, PA: IGI Global.

Burnes, T. R., Dexter, M. M., Richmond, K., Singh, A. A., and Cherrington, A. (2016) 'The Experiences of Transgender Survivors of Trauma Who Undergo Social and Medical Transition.' *Traumatology, 22*(1), 75–84. http://dx.doi.org/10.1037/trm0000064

Burnes, T. R. and Stanley, J. L. (2017) 'Introduction.' In T. R. Burnes and J. L. Stanley (eds) *Teaching LGBTQ+ Psychology: Queering Innovative Pedagogy and Practice* (pp.3–15). Washington, DC: American Psychological Association.

Burnes, T. R., Singh, A. A., and Witherspoon, R. G. (2017) 'Sex Positivity and Counseling Psychology: An Introduction to the Major Contribution.' *The Counseling Psychologist, 45*(4), 470–486. https://doi. org/10.1177/0011000017710216

Byne, W., Karasic, D. H., Coleman, E., Eyler, A. E. et al. (2018) 'Gender Dysphoria in Adults: An Overview and Primer for Psychiatrists.' *Transgender Health, 3,* 57–73. https://doi.org/10.1089/trgh.2017.0053

Carter, S. P., Allred, K. M., Tucker, R. P., Simpson, T. L., Shipherd, J. C., and Lehavot, K. (2019) 'Discrimination and Suicidal Ideation Among Transgender Veterans: The Role of Social Support and Connection.' *LGBT Health, 6*(2), 43–50. https://doi.org/10.1089/LGBT.2018.0239

Chang, S. C., Singh, A. A., and dickey, l. m. (2018) *A Clinician's Guide to Affirmative Practice: Working with Trans and Gender Nonbinary Clients.* Oakland, CA: Context Press.

Chen, D., Kyweluk, M. A., Sajwani, A., Gordon, E. J. et al. (2019) 'Factors Affecting Fertility Decision-Making Among Transgender Adolescents and Young Adults.' *LGBT Health, 6*(3), 107–115. https://doi.org/10.1089/ LGBT.2018.0250

Chen, J. A., Granato, H., Shipherd, J. C., Simpson, T., and Lehavot, K. (2017) 'A Qualitative Analysis of Transgender Veterans' Lived Experiences.' *Psychology of Sexual Orientation and Gender Diversity, 4*(1), 63–74. https://doi.org/10.1037/sgd0000217

Coleman, E., Bockting, W., Botzer, M., Cohen-Kettenis, P. et al. (2011) 'Standards of Care for the Health of Transsexual, Transgender, and Gender Nonconforming People.' *International Journal of Transgenderism, 13,* 165–232. https://doi.org/10.1080/15532739.2011.700873

Corrigan, P. W., Kosyluk, K. A., and Rüsch, N. (2013) 'Reducing Self-Stigma by Coming Out Proud.' *American Journal of Public Health, 103,* 794–800. https://doi.org/10.2105/AJPH.2012.301037

Crenshaw, K. (1991) 'Mapping the Margins: Intersectionality, Identity Politics, and Violence Against Women of Color.' *Stanford Law Review, 43*(6), 1241–1299. www.jstor.org/stable/1229039

Cronholm, P. F., Fogarty, C. T., Ambuel, B., and Harrison, S. L. (2011) 'Intimate Partner Violence.' *American Family Physician, 83*(10), 1165–1172.

Davenport v. DeRobertis, 844 F.2d 1310 (7th Cir 1988) No. 87–1233. Accessed on 05/13/2020 at https://casetext.com/case/davenport-v-derobertis-2

Davey, A., Arcelus, J., Meyer, C., and Bouman, W. P. (2015) 'Self-Injury Among Trans Individuals and Matched Controls: Prevalence and Associated Factors.' *Health and Social Care in the Community, 24*(4), 485–494. https://doi.org/10.1111/hsc.12239

Deutsch, M. B. and Buchholz, D. (2015) 'Electronic Health Records and Transgender Patients: Practical Recommendations for the Collection of Gender Identity Data.' *Journal of General Internal Medicine, 30,* 843–847. https://doi.org/10.1007/s11606-014-3148-7

Diamond, L. M. (2008) *Sexual Fluidity: Understanding Women's Love and Desire.* Cambridge, MA: Harvard University Press.

dickey, l. m. (2020a) 'Gender Nonbinary Mental Health.' In E. Rothblum (ed.) *The Oxford Handbook of Sexual and Gender Minority Mental Health.* Oxford: Oxford University Press.

dickey, l. m. (2020b) 'History of Gender Identity and Mental Health.' In E. Rothblum (ed.) *The Oxford Handbook of Sexual and Gender Minority Mental Health.* London: Oxford University Press.

dickey, l. m. and Budge, S. L. (2020) 'Suicide and the Transgender Experience: A Public Health Crisis.' *American Psychologist, 75*(3), 380–390. https://doi.org/10.1037/amp0000619

dickey, l. m., Budge, S. L., Katz-Wise, S. L., and Garza, M. V. (2016) 'Health Disparities in the Transgender Community: Exploring Differences in Insurance Coverage.' *Psychology of Sexual Orientation and Gender Diversity, 3*(3), 275–282. http://dx.doi.org/10.1037/sgd0000169

dickey, l. m., Ducheny, K. M., and Ehrbar, R. D. (2016) 'Family Creation Options for Transgender and Gender Nonconforming People.' *Psychology of Sexual Orientation and Gender Diversity, 3*(2), 173–179. http://dx.doi.org/10.1037/sgd0000178

dickey, l. m. and Loewy, M. I. (2010) 'Group Work with Transgender Clients.' *The Journal for Specialists in Group Work, 35*(3), 236–245. http://dx.doi.org/10.1080/01933922.2010.492904

dickey, l. m. and Singh, A. A. (2020) 'Evidence-Based Relationship Variable: Working with Trans and Gender Nonbinary Clients.' *Practice Innovations.* Advance Online Publication. http://dx.doi.org/10.1037/pri0000116

dickey, l. m., Reisner, S. L., and Juntunen, C. L. (2015) 'Non-Suicidal Self-Injury in a Large Online Sample of Transgender Adults.' *Professional Psychology: Research and Practice, 46*(1), 3–11. http://dx.doi.org/10.1037/a0038803

Dietert, M. and Dentice, D. (2015) 'The Transgender Military Experience: Their Battle for Workplace Rights.' *SAGE Open.* https://doi.org/10.1177/2158244015584231

Dietz, E. and Halem, J. (2016) 'Ethics Case: How Should Physicians Refer when Referral Options Are Limited for Transgender Patients?' *AMA Journal of Ethics, 18*(11), 1070–1078. https://doi.org/10.1001/journalofethics.2016.18.11.ecas1-1611

Dube, S. R., Anda, R. F., Felitti, V. J., Chapman, D. P., Williamson, D. F., and Giles, W. H. (2001) 'Childhood Abuse, Household Dysfunction, and the Risk of Attempted Suicide Throughout the Lifespan: Findings from the Adverse Childhood Experiences Study.' *JAMA, 286*(24), 3089–3096. https://doi.org/10.1001/jama.286.24.3089

Dysart-Gale, D. (2010) 'Social Justice and Social Determinants of Health: Lesbian, Gay, Bisexual, Transgendered, Intersexed, and Queer Youth in Canada.' *Journal of Child and Adolescent Psychiatric Nursing, 23*(1), 23–28. https://doi.org/10.1111/j.1744-6171.2009.00213.x

Ehrbar, R. D. and Gorton, R. N. (2010) 'Exploring Provider Treatment Models in Interpreting the *Standards of Care.' International Journal of Transgenderism, 12,* 198–210. https://doi.org/10.1080/15532739.2010.544235

Eleazer, J. R. (2016) 'Transgender Service Members and Veterans.' In N. Ainspan and C. Bryan (eds) *The Oxford Handbook of Psycho-Social Interventions for Veterans.* Oxford: Oxford University Press.

Eleazer, J. R. (2019) *'We've Been Here all Along': The Standpoint and Collective Resilience of Transgender U.S. Service Members* (Doctoral dissertation). University of Louisville, Louisville, KY. Retrieved from https://doi.org/10.18297/etd/3263

Espelage, D. L., Bosworth, K., and Simon, T. R. (2000) 'Examining the Social Context of Bullying Behaviors in Early Adolescence.' *Journal of Counseling and Development, 78,* 326–333. https://doi.org/10.1002/j.1556-6676.2000.tb01914.x

Felitti, V. J., Anda, R. F., Nordenberg, D., and Williamson, D. F. (1998) 'Relationship of Childhood Abuse and Household Dysfunction to Many of the Leading Causes of Death in Adults: The Adverse Childhood Experiences (ACE) Study.' *American Journal of Preventative Medicine, 14*(4), 245–258. https://doi.org/10.1016/S0749-3797(98)00017-8

Gates, G. J. and Herman, J. (2014) 'Transgender Military Service in the United States.' *The Williams Institute, UCLA.* Accessed on 05/13/2020 at https://escholarship.org/uc/item/1t24j53h

Genderbread person v 4.0. (n.d.) Home page. Accessed on 05/13/2020 at www.genderbread.org

Gilliam, J. E. (2013) *Gilliam Autism Rating Scale* (3rd ed.). San Antonio, TX: Pearson.

Glezer, A., McNiel, D. E., and Binder, R. L. (2013) 'Transgendered and Incarcerated: A Review of the Literature, Current Policies and Laws, and Ethics.' *Journal of the American Academy of Psychiatry and the Law, 41,* 551–559.

GLSEN and the National Center for Transgender Equality (2018) *Model School District Policy on Transgender and Gender Nonconforming Students: Model Language, Commentary, and Resources.* Accessed on 05/13/2020 at www.glsen.org/sites/default/files/Model-School-District-Policy-on-Transgender-and-Gender-Nonconforming-Students-GLSEN_0.pdf

Glynn, T. R., Garamel, K. E., Kahler, C. W., Iwamoto, M., Operario, D., and Nemoto, T. (2016) 'The Role of Gender Affirmation in Psychological Well-Being Among Transgender Women.' *Psychology of Sexual Orientation and Gender Diversity, 3*(3), 336–344. http://dx.doi.org/10.1037/sgd0000171

Goldblum, P., Testa, R. J., Pflum, S., Hendricks, M. L. et al. (2012) 'The Relationship Between Gender-Based Victimization and Suicide Attempts in Transgender People.' *Professional Psychology: Research and Practice, 43*(5), 468–475. https://doi.org/10.1037/a0029605

Goldstein, S. and Naglieri, J. A. (2009) *Autism Spectrum Rating Scale.* San Antonio, TX: Pearson.

Grant, J. M., Mottet, L. A., Tanis, J., Harrison, J., Herman, J. L., and Keisling, M. (2011) *Injustice at Every Turn: A Report of the National Transgender Discrimination Survey.* Washington, DC: National Center for Transgender Equality and National Gay and Lesbian Task Force.

Gregory, A., Cornell, D., Fan, X., and Sheras, P. (2010) 'Authoritative School Discipline: High School Practices Associated with Lower Bullying and Victimization.' *Journal of Educational Psychology, 102*(2), 483–496. https://doi.org/10.1037/a0018562

Grossman, A. H., Park, J. Y., and Russell, S. T. (2016) 'Transgender Youth and Suicidal Behaviours: Applying the Interpersonal Psychological Theory of Suicide.' *Journal of Gay & Lesbian Mental Health, 20,* 329–349. https://doi.org/10.1080/19359705.2016.1207581

Halcón, L. L. and Lifson, A. R. (2004) 'Prevalence and Predictors of Sexual Risks Among Homeless Youth.' *Journal of Youth and Adolescence, 33*(1), 71–80. https://doi.org/10.1023/A:1027338514930

Hatzenbuehler, M. L., Duncan, D., and Johnson, R. (2015) 'Neighborhood-Level LGBT Hate Crimes and Bullying Among Sexual Minority Youth: A Geospatial Analysis.' *Violence and Victims, 30*(4), 663–675. http://dx.doi.org/10.1891/0886-6708.VV-D-13-00166

Hatzenbuehler, M. L. and Pachankis, J. E. (2016) 'Stigma and Minority Stress as Social Determinants of Health Among Lesbian, Gay, Bisexual, and Transgender Youth: Research Evidence and Clinical Implications.' *Pediatric Clinics of North America, 63*(6), 985–997. http://dx.doi.org/10.1016/j.pcl.2016.07.003

Heck, N. C. (2017) 'Group Psychotherapy with Transgender and Gender Nonconforming Adults: Evidence-Based Practice Applications.' *Psychiatric Clinics of North America, 40,* 157–175. http://dx.doi.org/10.1016/j.psc.2016.10.010

Hendricks, M. L. and Testa, R. J. (2012) 'A Conceptual Framework for Clinical Work with Transgender and Gender Nonconforming Clients: An Adaptation of the Minority Stress Model.' *Professional Psychology: Research and Practice, 43*(5), 460–467. https://doi.org/10.1037/a0029597

Hendry, J. (1984) 'Shoes: The Early Learning of an Important Distinction in Japanese Society.' In G. Daniels (ed.) *Europe Interprets Japan.* Folkstone, England: Paul Norbury Publications. Accessed on 05/15/2020 at https://brill.com/view/book/9789004302877/B9789004302877_008.xml

Herman, J., Haas, A., and Rodgers, P. (2014) *Suicide Attempts Among Transgender and Gender Nonconforming Adults.* Los Angeles, CA: The Williams Institute, UCLA.

Hock, R. G. (2012) *Human Sexuality* (3rd ed.). Boston, MA: Pearson.

Institute of Medicine (2011) *The Health of Lesbian, Gay, Bisexual, and Transgender People: Building a Foundation for Better Understanding.* Washington, DC: The National Academies Press.

James S. E., Herman, J. L., Rankin, S., Keisling, M., Mottet, L., and Anafi, M. (2016) *The Report of the 2015 U.S. Transgender Survey.* Washington, DC: National Center for Transgender Equality. Accessed on 05/13/2020 at https://transequality.org/sites/default/files/docs/usts/USTS-Full-Report-Dec17.pdf

Johns, M. M., Beltran, O., Armstrong, H. L., Jayne, P. E., and Barrios, L. C. (2018) 'Protective Factors Among Transgender and Gender Variant Youth: A Systematic Review by Socioecological Level.' *Journal of Primary Prevention, 39,* 263–301. https://doi.org/10.1007/s10935-018-0508-9

Kattari, S. K. and Begun, S. (2017) 'On the Margins of Marginalized: Transgender Homelessness and Survival Sex.' *Journal of Women and Social Work, 32*(1), 92–103. https://doi.org/10.1177/0886109916651904

Keo-Meier, C. and Ehrensaft, D. (2018) 'Introduction to the Gender Affirmative Model.' In C. Keo-Meier and D. Ehrensaft (eds) *The Gender Affirmative Model: An Interdisciplinary Approach to Supporting Transgender and Gender Expansive Children* (pp.3–19). Washington, DC: American Psychological Association.

Kerrigan, M. F. (2012) 'Transgender Discrimination in the Military: The New Don't Ask, Don't Tell.' *Psychology, Public Policy, and Law 18*(3), 500–518. https://doi.org/10.1037/a0025771

Klonsky, E. D., Muehlenkamp, J. J., Lewis, S., and Walsh, B. W. (2011) *Advances in Psychotherapy: Nonsuicidal Self-Injury.* Cambridge, MA: Hogrefe Press.

Kuvalanka, K. A., Mahan, D. J., McGuire, J. K., and Hoffman, T. K. (2018) 'Perspectives of Mothers of Transgender and Gender-Nonconforming Children with Autism Spectrum Disorder.' *Journal of Homosexuality, 65*(9), 1167–1189. https://doi.org/10.1080/00918369.2017.1406221

Lambda Legal (n.d.) *Glenn v. Brumby et al.* Accessed on 05/17/2020 at www.lambdalegal.org/in-court/cases/glenn-v-brumby-et-al

Levine, S. B. (2016) 'Reflections of the Legal Battles Over Prisoners with Gender Dysphoria.' *Journal of the American Academy of Psychiatry and the Law, 44*, 236–245.

Library of Congress (2016) *The Civil Rights Act of 1964: A Long Struggle for Freedom.* Accessed on 06/15/2020 at www.loc.gov/exhibits/civil-rights-act/index.html

Linehan, M. M. (2015a) *DBT Skills Training Handouts and Worksheets* (2nd ed.). New York, NY: Guilford Press.

Linehan, M. M. (2015b) *DBT Skills Training Manual* (2nd ed.). New York, NY: Guilford Press.

Littman, L. (2018) 'Parent Reports of Adolescents and Young Adults Perceived to Show Signs of Rapid Onset Gender Dysphoria.' *PLoS ONE, 13*(8), e0202330. https://doi.org/10.1371/journal.pone.0202330

Maddux, S. (Director) (2010) *Gen Silent* [Film]. Interrobang Productions. San Rafael, CA: 32TEN Studios.

Marchiano, L. (2017) 'Outbreak: on Transgender Teens and Psychic Epidemics.' *Psychological Perspectives, 60*(3), 345–633. https://doi.org/10.1080/00332925.2017.1350804

Marshall, E., Claes, L., Bouman, W. P., Witcomb, G. L., and Arcelus, J. (2016) 'Non-Suicidal Self-Injury and Suicidality in Trans People: A Systematic Review of the Literature.' *International Review of Psychiatry, 28*(1), 58–69. https://doi.org/10.3109/09540261.2015.1073143

Maslow, A. H. (1943) 'A Theory of Human Motivation.' *Psychological Review, 50*(4), 370–396. https://doi.org/10.1037/h0054346

Meyer, I. H. (1995) 'Minority Stress and Mental Health in Gay Men.' *Journal of Health and Social Behavior, 36*(1), 38–56. http://www.jstor.org/stable/2137286

Meyer, I. H. (2013) 'Prejudice, Social Stress, and Mental Health in Lesbian, Gay, and Bisexual Populations: Conceptual Issues and Research Evidence.' *Psychology of Sexual Orientation and Gender Diversity, 1*(S), 3–26. https://doi.org/10.1037/0033-2909.129.5.674

Morris, E. R. and Galupo, M. P. (2019) '"Attempting to Dull the Dysphoria": Nonsuicidal Self-Injury Among Transgender Individuals.' *Psychology of Sexual Orientation and Gender Diversity, 6*, 296–307. https://doi.org/10.1037/sgd0000327

Movement Advancement Project (2020) *Snapshot: LGBTQ Equality by State.* Accessed on 05/15/2020 at www.lgbtmap.org/equality-maps

Muehlenkamp, J. J. (2012) 'Body Regard in Non-Suicidal Self-Injury: Theoretical Explanations and Treatment Decisions.' *Journal of Cognitive Psychotherapy, 26,* 331–347. https://doi.org/10.1891/0889-8391.26.4.331

Nadal, K. L. (2013) *That's So Gay! Microaggressions and the Lesbian, Gay, Bisexual, and Transgender Community.* Washington, DC: American Psychological Association. https://doi.org/10.1037/14093-000

National Center for Transgender Equality, Transgender American Veterans Association Service Members, Partners, Allies Respect and Tolerance for All OutServe: Servicemembers Legal Defense Network and The American Military Partner Association (n.d.) 'Military Service by Transgender People: Data from the 2015 U.S. Transgender Survey.' Accesed on 05/13/2020 at https://www.transequality.org/sites/default/files/docs/usts/USTS-VeteransDayReport.pdf

National Center for Transgender Equality (2014) *The WHO Report: Decriminalize Sex Work, Drug Use to Prevent Spread of HIV.* Accessed on 05/13/2020 at https://transequality.org/blog/new-who-report-decriminalize-sex-work-drug-use-to-prevent-spread-of-hiv

National Center for Transgender Equality (2020a) *Federal Case Law on Transgender People and Discrimination.* Accessed on 05/17/2020 at https://transequality.org/federal-case-law-on-transgender-people-and-discrimination

National Center for Transgender Equality (2020b) *Selective Service and Transgender People.* Accessed on 05/13/2020 at https://transequality.org/issues/resources/selective-service-and-transgender-people

National PREA Resource Center (2020) *Prison Rape Elimination Act.* Accessed on 05/13/2020 at www.prearesourcecenter.org/about/prison-rape-elimination-act-prea

Nelson, L. (2016) '5 Maps that Show How Sex Education in the US Is Failing.' *Vox.* Accessed on 05/15/2020 at www.vox.com/2016/1/10/10738766/sex-ed-states-maps

Norquist, D. L. (2019) *Directive-type Memorandum (DTM)-19-004: Military Service by Transgender Persons with Gender Dysphoria.* Accessed on 05/13/2020 at www.esd.whs.mil/Portals/54/Documents/DD/issuances/dtm/DTM%2019-004.PDF?ver=2020-03-17-140438-090

Obedin-Maliver, J., Goldsmith, E. S., Stewart, L., White, W. et al. (2011) 'Lesbian, Gay, Bisexual, Transgender-Related Content in Undergraduate Medical Education.' *JAMA, 306,* 971–977. https://doi.org/10.1001/jama.2011.1255

Obergefell et al. v. Hodges (2015) No. 14-556. Accessed on 05/17/2020 at www.supremecourt.gov/opinions/14pdf/14-556_3204.pdf

Olson, K. R., Durwood, L., DeMeules, M., and McLaughlin, K. A. (2016) 'Mental Health of Transgender Children Who Are Supported in Their Identities.' *Pediatrics, 137*(3), 1–8. https://doi.org/10.1542/peds.2015-3223

Oransky, M., Burke, E., and Steever, J. (2019) 'An Interdisciplinary Model for Meeting the Needs of Transgender Adolescents and Young Adults: The Mount Sinai Adolescent Health Center Approach.' *Cognitive and Behavioral Practice, 26*(4), 603–616. https://doi.org/10.1016/j.cbpra.2018.03.002

Owen-Smith, A.A., Gerth, J., Sineath, R. C., Barzilay, J. et al. (2018) 'Association Between Gender Confirmation Treatments and Perceived Gender Congruence, Body Image Satisfaction and Mental Health in a Cohort of Transgender Individuals.' *Journal of Sexual Medicine, 15*, 591–600. https://doi.org/10.1016/j.jsxm.2018.01.017

Parco, J. E., Levy, D. A., and Spears, S. R. (2015) 'Transgender Military Personnel in the Post-DADT Repeal Era: A Phenomenological Study.' *Armed Forces & Society, 41*(2), 221–242. https://doi.org/10.1177/0095327X14530112

Pederson, L. and Pederson, C. (2017) *The Expanded Dialectical Behavior Therapy Skills Training Manual: DBT for Self-Help and Individual and Group Treatment Settings* (2nd ed.). Eau Claire, WI: PESI Publishing and Media.

Pega, F. and Veale, J. F. (2015) 'The Case for the World Health Organization's Commission on Social Determinants of Health to Address Gender Identity.' *American Journal of Public Health, 105*(3), e58–e62. https://doi.org/10.2105/ajph.2014.302373

Peterson, C. M., Matthews, A., Copps-Smith, E., and Conard, L. A. (2017) 'Suicidality, Self-Harm, and Body Dissatisfaction in Transgender Adolescents and Emerging Adults with Gender Dysphoria.' *Suicide and Life-Threatening Behavior, 47*, 475–482. https://doi.org/10.1111/sltb.12289

Pew Research Center (2015) *America's Changing Religious Landscape.* Accessed on 05/13/2020 at www.pewforum.org/2015/05/12/americas-changing-religious-landscape

Prison Rape Elimination Act, 34 USC Ch. 303 (2003) Chapter 303. Accessed on 05/13/2020 at https://uscode.house.gov/view.xhtml?path=/prelim@title34/subtitle3/chapter303&edition=prelim

Puckett, J. A. (2019) 'An Ecological Approach to Therapy with Gender Minorities.' *Cognitive and Behavioral Practice, 26*(4), 647–655. https://doi.org/10.1016/j.cbpra.2019.08.002

Puckett, J. A., Cleary, P., Rossman, K., Newcomb, M. E., and Mustanski, B. (2018) 'Barriers to Gender-Affirming Care for Transgender and Gender Nonconforming Individuals.' *Sex Research and Social Policy, 15*(1), 48–59. https://doi.org/10.1007/s13178-017-0295-8

Reisner, S. L., Greytak, E. A., Parsons, J. T., and Ybarra, M. L. (2015) 'Gender Minority Social Stress in Adolescence: Disparities in Adolescent Bullying and Substance Use by Gender Identity.' *Journal of Sex Research, 52*(3), 243–256. https://doi.org/10.1080/00224499.2014.886321

Reuter, T. R., Newcomb, M. E., Whitton, S. W., and Mustanski, B. (2017) 'Intimate Partner Violence Victimization in LGBTQ+ Young Adults: Demographic Differences and Associations with Health Behaviors.' *Psychology of Violence, 7*(1), 101–109. https://doi.org/10.1037/vio0000031

Richmond, K. A., Burnes, T., and Carroll, K. (2012) 'Lost in Trans-Lation: Interpreting Systems of Trauma for Transgender Clients.' *Traumatology, 18*(1), 45–57. https://doi.org/10.1177/1534765610396726

Richmond, K., Burnes, T. R., Singh, A. A., and Ferrara, M. (2017) 'Assessment and Treatment of Trauma with TGNC Clients: A Feminist Approach.' In A. A. Singh and l. m. dickey (eds) *Affirmative Counseling and Psychological Practice with Transgender and Gender Nonconforming Clients* (pp.191–212). Washington, DC: American Psychological Association.

Rogers, C. R. (1961) *On Becoming a Person: A Therapist's View of Psychotherapy.* New York, NY: Houghton Mifflin.

Rood, B. A., Reisner, S. L., Puckett, J. A., Surace, F. I., Berman, A. K., and Pantalone, D. W. (2017) 'Internalized Transphobia: Exploring Perceptions of Social Messages in Transgender and Gender-Nonconforming Adults.' *International Journal of Transgenderism, 18*(4), 411–426. https://doi.org/10.1080/15532739.2017.1329048

Ryan, C., Russell, S. T., Huebner, D., Diaz, R., and Sanchez, J. (2010) 'Family Acceptance in Adolescence and the Health of LGBT Young Adults.' *Journal of Child and Adolescent Psychiatric Nursing, 23*(4), 205–213. https://doi.org/10.1111/j.1744-6171.2010.00246.x

Santo, A. (2018) *Prison Rape Allegations on the Rise: But the Accusations Are Still Rarely Found to Be True.* Accessed on 05/13/2020 at www.themarshallproject.org/2018/07/25/prison-rape-allegations-are-on-the-rise

Schopler, E., Van Bourgondien, M. E., Wellman, G. J., and Love, S. R. (2010) *Childhood Autism Rating Scale* (2nd ed.). San Antonio, TX: Pearson.

Shipherd, J. C., Mizock, L., Maguen, S., and Green, K. E. (2012) 'Male-to-Female Transgender Veterans and VA Healthcare Utilization.' *International Journal of Sexual Health, 24*(1), 78–87. https://doi.org//10.1080/19317611.2011.639440

Singh, A. A. (2013) 'Transgender Youth of Color and Resilience: Negotiating Oppression and Finding Support.' *Sex Roles, 68*, 690–702. https://doi.org/10.1007/s11199-012-0149-z

Singh, A. A. and dickey, l. m. (2017) 'Introduction.' In A. A. Singh and l. m. dickey (eds) *Affirmative Counseling and Psychological Practice with Transgender and Gender Nonconforming Clients* (pp.3–18). Washington, DC: American Psychological Association.

Singh, A. A., Hays, D. G., and Watson, L. S. (2011) 'Strength in the Face of Adversity: Resilience Strategies of Transgender Individuals.' *Journal of Counseling & Development, 89*(1), 20–27. https://doi.org/10.1002/j.1556-6678.2011.tb00057.x

Southwick, S. M., Bonanno, G. A., Masten, A. S., Panter-Brick, C., and Yehuda, R. (2014) 'Resilience Definitions, Theory, and Challenges: Interdisciplinary Perspectives.' *European Journal of Traumatology, 5.* http://dx.doi.org/10.3402/ejpt.v5.25338

Strang, J. F., Meagher, H., Kenworthy, L., de Vries, A. L. C. et al. (2016) 'Initial Clinical Guidelines for Co-Occurring Autism Spectrum Disorder and Gender Dysphoria on Incongruence in Adolescents.' *Journal of Clinical Child & Adolescent Psychology, 47*(1), 105–115. https://doi.org/10.1080/15374416.2016.1228462

Tebbe, E. A. and Moradi, B. (2016) 'Suicide Risk in Trans Populations: An Application of Minority Stress Theory.' *Journal of Counseling Psychology, 63*(5), 520–533. https://doi.org/10.1037/cou0000152

Temple-Newhook J., Pyne J., Winters K., Feder S. et al. (2018) 'A Critical Commentary on Follow-up Studies and "Desistance" Theories about Transgender and Gender Non-Conforming Children.' *International Journal of Transgenderism, 19*(2), 212–224. https://doi.org/10.1080/15532739.2018.1456390

Toomey, R. B., Syvertsen, A. K., and Shramko, M. (2018) 'Transgender Adolescent Suicide Behavior.' *Pediatrics, 142*, 1–8. https://doi.org/10.1542/peds.2017-4218

U.S. Department of Health and Human Services (2019) *Ryan White HIV/AIDS Program Legislation.* Accessed on 05/13/2020 at https://hab.hrsa.gov/about-ryan-white-hivaids-program/ryan-white-hivaids-program-legislation

U.S. Department of Health and Human Services (2020) *Fact Sheet: HHS Finalizes ACA Section 1557 Rule.* Accessed on 06/15/2020 at www.hhs.gov/sites/default/files/1557-final-rule-factsheet.pdf

Wadman, M. (2018) '"Rapid Onset" of Transgender Identity Ignites Storm.' *Science, 361*(6406), 958–959. https://doi.org/10.1126/science.361.6406.958

Wahlig, J. L. (2015) 'Losing the Child They Thought They Had: Therapeutic Suggestions for an Ambiguous Loss Perspective with Parents of a Transgender Child.' *Journal of GLBT Studies, 11*, 305–326. http://dx.doi.org/10.1080/1550428X.2014.945676

Walker, J. K. (2015) 'Investigating Trans People's Vulnerabilities to Intimate Partner Violence/Abuse.' *Partner Abuse, 6*(1), 107–125. http://dx.doi.org/10.1891/1946-6560.6.1.107

Warren, J. C., Smalley, K. B., and Barefoot, N. (2016) 'Psychological Well-Being Among Transgender and Genderqueer Individuals.' *International Journal of Transgenderism, 17*(3–4), 114–123. http://dx.doi.org/10.1080/15532739.2016.1216344

White, T. and Ettner, R. (2004) 'Disclosure, Risks and Protective Factors for Children Whose Parents Are Undergoing a Gender Transition.' *Journal of Gay & Lesbian Psychotherapy, 8*, 129–147. DOI: 10.1300/J236v08n01_10

White, T. and Ettner, R. (2007) 'Adaptation and Adjustment in Children of Transsexual Parents.' *European Child & Adolescent Psychiatry, 16*, 215–221. http://dx.doi.org/10.1007/s00787-006-0591-y

White Hughto, J. M. and Clark, K. A. (2019) 'Designing a Transgender Health Training for Correctional Healthcare Providers: A Feasibility Study.' *The Prison Journal, 99*(3), 329–342. https://doi.org/10.1177/0032885519837237

Wilson, E. C., Garofalo, R., Harris, R. D., Herrick, A. et al. (2009) 'Transgender Female Youth and Sex Work: HIV Risk and a Comparison of Life Factors Related to Engagement in Sex Work.' *AIDS and Behavior, 13*, 902–913. https://doi.org/10.1007/s10461-008-9508-8

Winters, K. and Ehrbar, R. D. (2010) 'Beyond Conundrum: Strategies for Diagnostic Harm Reduction.' *Journal of Gay and Lesbian Mental Health, 14*, 130–138. https://doi.org/10.1080/19359701003609922

Woodrum, T. D. (2019) *The Relationship Between Demoralization, Community Connectedness, and Well-Being Among Transgender and Gender Diverse Individuals*. Santa Barbara, CA: Fielding Graduate Institute.

Yanos, P. T., Roe, D., and Lysaker, P. H. (2011) 'Narrative Enhancement and Cognitive Therapy: A New Group-Based Treatment for Internalized Stigma Among Persons with Severe Mental Illness.' *International Journal of Group Psychotherapy, 61*, 576–595. https://dx.doi.org/10.1521/ijgp.2011.61.4.576

Further Reading and Other Resources

Becoming an Ally to the Gender-Expansive Child: A Guide for Parents and Carers by Anna Bianchi

Becoming Nicole: The Transformation of an American Family by Amy Ellis Nutt

Beyond Magenta: Transgender Teens Speak Out by Susan Kuklin

Born on the Edge of Race and Gender: A Voice for Cultural Competency by Willy Wilkinson

Butch is a Noun by S. Bear Bergman

The Conscious Parent's Guide to Gender Identity: A Mindful Approach to Embracing Your Child's Authentic Self by Darlene Tando

Families in Transition: Parenting Gender Diverse Children, Adolescents, and Young Adults by Arlene I. Lev and Andrew R. Gottlieb

Gender Born, Gender Made: Raising Healthy Gender-Nonconforming Children by Diane Ehrensaft

Gender Creative Child: Pathways for Nurturing and Supporting Children Who Live Outside Gender Boxes by Diane Ehrensaft and Norman Spack

The Gender Identity Workbook for Kids: A Guide to Exploring Who You Are by Kelly Storck and Noah Grigni

Gender Outlaws: The Next Generation by Kate Bornstein and S. Bear Bergman

The Gender Quest Workbook: A Guide for Teens and Young Adults Exploring Gender Identity by Rylan Jay Testa, Deborah Coolhart, and Jayme Peta

Gracefully Grayson by Ami Polonsky

Hung Jury: Testimonies of Genital Surgery by Transsexual Men by Trystan T. Cotten

Invisible Lives: The Erasure of Transsexual and Transgendered People by Vivane K. Namaste

Journeys of Transformation: Stories from Across the Acronym by Reid Vanderburgh

The Last Time I Wore a Dress: A Memoir by Daphne Scholinski

The Lives of Transgender People by Genny Beemyn and Susan Rankin

Lou Sullivan: Daring to be a Man Among Men by Brice D. Smith

Manning Up: Transsexual Men on Finding Brotherhood, Family and Themselves by Zander Keig and Mitch Kellaway

My Son Wears Heels: One Mom's Journey from Clueless to Kickass by Julie Tarney

Normal Life: Administrative Violence, Critical Trans Politics, and the Limits of the Law by Dean Spade

Now What? A Handbook for Families with Transgender Children by Rex Butt

On the Couch with Dr. Angello: A Guide to Raising and Supporting Transgender Youth by Michele Angello

Polyamory: The New Love Without Limits: Secrets of Sustainable Intimate Relationships by Deborah M. Anapol

The Queer and Transgender Resilience Workbook: Skills for Navigating Sexual Orientation and Gender Expression by Anneliese A. Singh

Redefining Realness: My Path to Womanhood, Identity, Love, and So Much More by Janet Mock

Rethinking Normal: A Memoir in Transition by Katie Rain Hill

Right Mind Wrong Body: The Ultimate TRANS Guide to Being Complete and Living a Fulfilling Life by Neo L. Sandja

Second Son: Transitioning Toward My Destiny, Love and Life by Ryan K. Sallans

Some Assembly Required: The Not-So-Secret Life of a Transgender Teen by Arin Andrews

Stuck in the Middle with You: A Memoir of Parenting in Three Genders by Jennifer Finney Boylan

Trans Bodies, Trans Selves: A Resource for the Transgender Community by L. Erickson-Schroth

Transforming Manhood: A Trans Man's Quest to Build Bridges and Knock Down Walls by Ryan K. Sallans

Transgender 101: A Simple Guide to a Complex Issue by Nicholas M. Teich

The Transgender Child: A Handbook for Families and Professionals by Stephanie Brill and Rachel Pepper

Transgender Family Law: A Guide to Effective Advocacy by Jennifer L. Levi and Elizabeth E. Monnin-Browder

Transgender Sex Work and Society by Larry Nuttbrock

The Transgender Teen: A Handbook for Parents and Professionals Supporting Transgender and Non-Binary Teens by Stephanie Brill and Lisa Kenney

Transition and Beyond: Observations on Gender Identity by Reid Vanderburgh

Trans: Transgender Life Stories from South Africa by Ruth Morgan, Charl Marais, and Joy Rosemary Wellbeloved

Transitions of the Heart: Stories of Love, Struggle and Acceptance by Mothers of Transgender and Gender Variant Children by Rachel Pepper

Travesti: Sex, Gender, and Culture Among Brazilian Transgendered Prostitutes by Don Kulick

Treating Transgender Children and Adolescents by Jack Drescher and William Byne

What Becomes You by Aaron Raz Link and Hilda Raz

Where's MY Book? A Guide for Transgender and Gender Non-Conforming Youth, Their Parents, and Everyone Else by Linda Gromko

Whipping Girl: A Transsexual Woman on Sexism and the Scapegoating of Femininity by Julia Serano

Wrapped in Blue: A Journey of Discovery by Donna Rose

You and Your Gender Identity: A Guide to Discovery by Dara Hoffman-Fox

Subject Index

abandonment schema 147–8
access/custody (for trans
    parents) 137
adolescents
  bullying 83–9
  non-binary identities 74–82
  nonsuicidal self-injury
      (NSSI) 66–73
  puberty 59–65
  sense of self 72
  sexuality exploration 100–6
  social media 90–9
adoption/fostering 63, 119
adultism 40
Adverse Childhood
    Experiences (ACES) 95
advocating for clients
    88–9, 163–72
affirmative practice 24, 169–72
Allen, Christopher 14, 142
Angello, Michele 19, 41
autism spectrum disorder (ASD)
  accommodations 43
  assessment of 45, 48

"autism in women"
    phenomenon 47–8
gender identity, and 44, 47–8
guidelines for working with
    trans youth 44–5
interdisciplinary team 45
stigmatization 46
treatment goals for 47

blood tests 95
body dissatisfaction 63, 68, 71
broken arm syndrome 171
buddy system 76–7
bullying 83–9

cell phone use 94, 96, 97–8
Cerezo, Alison 13
chest development 63
chest feeding 120
children
  age at which clear about
      identity 33
  bullying 83–9
  custody/access (for trans
      parents) 137

children *cont.*
  Gender Affirmative Model
    (GAM) with 32–3
  mixed parental support
    for 50–5
  parents coming out to 136–42
  secrecy and 30, 34
  speaking directly with 30
  support and outcomes 27, 50
  terminology used by 27
  "watchful waiting"
    with 31, 33, 34
  working with pre-
    school-aged 31–2
  see also school
cisgender
  definition 22
  normativity of 103–4
  partner 150–5
concrete thinking 55
congruence 142
consent to treatment
  (from parents) 75
coping skills 68, 71
couples counseling 150–5
cultural alignment 115
cultural humility 88, 104
cultural values 28–9, 32, 33
custody/access (for trans
  parents) 137
cutting 66–73

DBT skills 68
decision-making (shared) 170–1
demoralization 70–1
desistance 81–2
detransitioning 82

discrimination in the
  workplace 111
Don't Ask, Don't Tell policy 132
Ducheny, Kelly 16–7, 121

Edwards-Leeper, Laura 18, 55
Eleazer, Jacob 15, 134
employee evaluations 110, 115–6
experience/knowledge
  (counselor's) 60, 101–2,
    105, 126, 171–2

family
  evaluating the family
    system 80
  extended 33–4
  see also children; parents
fertility concerns 63, 78–9
"flight to masculinity" 114
fluidity of gender 32, 33, 55
forms/paperwork (intake)
  130, 134, 164, 166–7
fostering/adopting 63, 119
functional analysis 72

gatekeeper model 21
gender
  definition 22
  sex and 103
Gender Affirmative Model
  (GAM) 31–2
gender binary 23
gender dysphoria 31, 45, 79
gender identity
  conflated with sexual
    identity 53
  definition 23

gender identity disorder diagnosis 31
Gender and Sexuality Alliance (GSA) 75, 76
gender-affirming care 169–72
Genderbread Person 53
genograms 28
Giammattei, Shawn V. 20, 34
Glenn, Vandy Beth 111
Gonzalez, Cesar A. 14, 172
Gratton, Finn V. 14–5
Green, Addis 13
grief 146
Gromko, Linda 18, 65
grooming 96–7

harm-reduction approach 95
health insurance 112–3
Hendricks, Michael L. 18, 155
hierarchy of needs 70
history taking 170
homelessness 91–7, 124
homophobia 29–30, 54
Hopwood, Ruben 19–20
hormones
    harm-reduction approach and 95
    stopping 118

in-patient mental health facility 156–62
Indigenous cultures 74, 79
Individualized Education Plan (IEP) 43, 47
institutional settings 156–62
intersecting identities

cumulative effect of 44, 122–7
political intersectionality 123
race 122
representational intersectionality 123
structural intersectionality 122
Inuit nation 83–9
involuntary discharge (military) 133

jails 160–1
Jourdan, Mira 19, 126

knowledge/experience (counselor's) 60, 101–2, 105, 126, 171–2

lab tests 95
legislation
    fostering/adopting 119
    prisons 160–1
    service members 128–9
    workplace 111, 116
locker rooms 112

Marchant, Landon 17–8
"mayhem" laws 21
medical care
    mental health provider's role 167–8
    non-affirmative practice 157–8, 163–5
    organ systems treated 167
    patient-centered care 169–72
medical facilities 156–62

medical mistrust 171
menstruation 68, 71
mental health facility 156–62
military service *see*
    service members
minority stress theory
    (MST) 70–1, 171
misgendering 62, 65
Morsa, Benjamin 14
Muehlenkamp, Jennifer J. 15

Nadal, Kevin 17, 89
name changes 112
negative religious coping 147
nicknames 112
non-binary identities
    23–4, 74–82
nonsuicidal self-injury
    (NSSI) 66–73

Pankey, Tyson L. 20, 172
pansexuality 101, 105
paperwork/forms (intake)
    130, 134, 164, 166–7
parenting
    adoption/fostering 63, 119
    becoming a trans
        parent 117–21
    future plans 63, 78–9
    surrogate pregnancy 120
parents
    coming out to children 136–42
    concerns of 29–30, 37–8, 54
    conflict between 29, 50–5
    consent to medical
        treatment 75

creating safe inner
    circle 38, 40–1
defensiveness from 51
developing rapport with 54
"have done something
    wrong" 32, 37
internalized stigma 46, 48
shame felt by 33
partner (cisgender) 150–5
patient-centered care 169–72
phone use 94, 96, 97–8
physical exams 170
political intersectionality 123
polyamorous identity 101–2, 105
"preferred pronoun" 167
prisons 160–1
pronouns (mistakes with) 62, 65
puberty 59–65
puberty blockers 62–5, 78, 118

"rapid onset gender
    dysphoria" 81
references (for work) 113–4
referrals
    appropriate 172
    sample letters 177–9
rejecting schema 147–8
religious values 143–9
representational
    intersectionality 123
resilience 70, 125
restrooms 112, 132, 135
retraining 114
Rossman, Kinton 17, 80

safety planning 76
school
    Gender and Sexuality
        Alliance (GSA) 75, 76
    health education class 44
    Individualized Education
        Plan (IEP) 43, 47
    *Model School District
        Policy* document 40
    other students 38–9
    playground environment 39
    preparation at (before
        coming out) 41
    sex education 103
    working with administrators
        39–40
secrecy 30, 34
segregation (in prison) 160–1
selective service 122–3
self-actualization 70
self-injury 66–73
service members 51–2,
    122–3, 128–35
sex education 103
sex (vs. gender) 103
sex work 90–1, 123, 124
sex-positive approach 104
sexual history taking 170
sexual identity
    conflated with gender
        identity 53
    definition 23
sexual orientation options 100
sexuality exploration 100–6
shame (parents') 33
"she-males" 123
social contagion effect 81

social determinants of
    health (SDOH) 69
social isolation 69, 72, 77
social media 90–9
social support 77
solitary confinement 160–1
spectrum (gender as a) 32
Spencer, Katie 16
Status Information Letter
    (SIL) 122–3
stigma
    autism spectrum disorder 46
    internalized 46, 48
STOP skills 68
structural intersectionality 122
suicidal thinking 66–73
supervisor's experience 73
support, potential loss of 141
surrogate pregnancy 120
survival sex 90–1, 123, 124
systems perspective 158–60

Tanner Stages 78
technology access 94, 96
terminology 22–4
trans (definition) 23
transactional sex 90–1, 123, 124
transgender (definition) 22
transsexual (definition) 23
trauma-informed treatment
    98–9, 171

uniforms (in workplace) 112

VA healthcare 134
values (origins of) 146
Vencill, Jennifer A. 15, 106

"watchful waiting" (with
    children) 31, 33, 34
workplace
    assessing climate of 114
    career counseling 116
    discrimination in 111
    employee evaluations
        110, 115–6

health insurance 112–3
legislation 111, 116
locker rooms 112
references 113–4
restrooms 112
uniforms 112

Author Index

Achenbach, T. 49
Adelson, J. L. 142
Agency for Healthcare
    Research and Quality 171
American Psychiatric
    Association 31, 42, 79
American Psychological
    Association 22, 24,
    32, 103, 105, 172
APAGS Committee on
    Sexual Orientation and
    Gender Diversity 114
Aragon, S. R. 89
Arcelus, J. 71
Ashley, F. 81

Barefoot, N. 142
Baril, A. 81
Barr, S. M. 142
Baus, J. 160
Begun, S. 90, 91
Benjamin, H. 23, 100
Binder, R. L. 162
Blosnich, J. R. 69
Bosworth, K. 89

Bouman, W. P. 71
Buchholz, D. 95
Budge, S. L. 69, 72, 142
Bureau of Justice Statistics 161
Burke, E. 72
Burnes, T. R. 77, 98, 104, 127
Byne, W. 165

Carroll, K. 77, 98, 127
Carter, S. P. 134
Chang, S. C. 23, 24, 70, 171
Chen, D. 120
Chen, J. A. 132
Clark, K. A. 161
Coleman, E. 106, 127
Cornell, D. 83
Corrigan, P. W. 72
Crenshaw, K. 122, 123
Cronholm, P. F. 77

Davenport v. DeRobertis 160
Davey, A. 71
Dentice, D. 132
Deutsch, M. B. 95
Diamond, L. M. 100

dickey, l. m. 21, 23, 24, 32, 49, 66, 69, 71, 72, 77, 78, 120
Dietert, M. 132
Dietz, E. 95, 127
Dube, S. R. 125
Ducheny, K. M. 78, 120, 121
Duncan, D. 89
Dysart-Gale, D. 69

Ehrbar, R. D. 78, 95, 120
Ehrensaft, D. 31, 32
Eleazer, J. R. 132, 133, 134
Espelage, D. L. 89
Ettner, R. 137

Fan, X. 83
Felitti, V. J. 95
Ferrara, M. 77

Galupo, M. P. 71
Garza, M. V. 69
Gates, G. J. 128
genderbread.org 53
Gilliam, J. E. 45
Glezer, A. 162
GLSEN 39, 83
Glynn, T. R. 142
Goldblum, P. 70
Goldstein, S. 45
Gorton, R. N. 95
Grant, J. M. 69, 163
Green, K. E. 128
Gregory, A. 83, 88, 89
Grossman, A. H. 71

Haas, A. 71
Halcón, L. L. 94, 97
Halem, J. 95, 127
Hatzenbuehler, M. L. 69, 89
Hays, D. G. 70
Heck, N. C. 77
Hendricks, M. L. 70, 171
Hendry, J. 28
Herman, J. 71, 128
Hock, R. G. 100
Hunt, D. 160

Institute of Medicine 169

James S. E. 66, 69, 123, 134, 163, 164
Johns, M. M. 72
Johnson, R. 89
Juntunen, C. L. 66, 71

Kattari, S. K. 90, 91
Katz-Wise, S. L. 69
Keo-Meier, C. 31, 32
Kerrigan, M. F. 132
Klonsky, E. D. 72
Kosyluk, K. A. 72
Kuvalanka, K. A. 44

Lambda Legal 111
Levine, S. B. 161
Levy, D. A. 133
Library of Congress 111
Lifson, A. R. 94, 97
Linehan, M. M. 67, 68, 72
Littman, L. 81

Loewy, M. I. 77
Lysaker, P. H. 72

McNiel, D. E. 162
Maddux, S. 156
Maguen, S. 128
Marchiano, L. 81
Marshall, E. 72
Maslow, A. H. 70
Meyer, I. H. 70, 71
Mizock, L. 128
Moradi, B. 70
Morris, E. R. 71
Movement Advancement
    Project 119
Muehlenkamp, J. J. 71

Nadal, K. L. 123
Naglieri, J. A. 45
National Center for Transgender
    Equality (NCTE) 39, 83,
    111, 122, 123, 129
National PREA Resource
    Center 161
Nelson, L. 103
Norquist, D. L. 129

Obedin-Maliver, J. 163
Obergefell et al. v. Hodges 119
Olson, K. R. 27, 50
Oransky, M. 72
Owen-Smith, A. A. 71

Pachankis, J. E. 69
Parco, J. E. 132
Park, J. Y. 71

Pederson, C. 67, 72
Pederson, L. 67, 72
Pega, F. 69
Peterson, C. M. 71
Pew Research Center 143
Puckett, J. A. 72, 73

Reisner, S. L. 66, 71, 89
Reuter, T. R. 77
Richmond, K. A. 77, 98, 127
Rodgers, P. 71
Roe, D. 72
Rogers, C. R. 142
Rood, B. A. 72
Rüsch, N. 72
Russell, S. T. 71
Ryan, C. 27, 50

Santo, A. 161
Schopler, E. 45
Sheras, P. 83
Shipherd, J. C. 128
Shramko, M. 71
Simon, T. R. 89
Singh, A. A. 23, 24, 40, 49,
    70, 77, 104, 125
Smalley, K. B. 142
Southwick, S. M. 125
Spears, S. R. 133
Stanley, J. L. 104
Steever, J. 72
Strang, J. F. 42, 44, 45
Syvertsen, A. K. 71

Tebbe, E. A. 70
Temple-Newhook J. 82

Testa, R. J. 70, 171
Toomey, R. B. 71

U.S. Department of Health and
    Human Services 116, 123

Veale, J. F. 69

Wadman, M. 81
Wahlig, J. L. 146
Walker, J. K. 77

Warren, J. C. 142
Watson, L. S. 70
White Hughto, J. M. 161
White, T. 137
Williams, R. 160
Wilson, E. C. 90
Winters, K. 95
Witherspoon, R. G. 104
Woodrum, T. D. 70

Yanos, P. T. 72